How selling your home
can be the most *blissful*
time of your life

Natalie Evans

Rethink

First published in Great Britain in 2022
by Rethink Press (www.rethinkpress.com)

Cover photograph by La Boheme Photography

Contents

Introduction

Whether you are already selling your home or starting to plan your future home sale, I am delighted that together we are going to make your home sale one of the happiest journeys of your life. It's said that selling your home is one of the most stressful times you'll ever experience – in the media, in conversation with those who have been through it – so it's not surprising that we struggle to see the truly inspiring journey that lies ahead. One survey by *Which?* Mortgage Advisors found that 70% of people find buying or selling a home stressful, putting it second only to divorce as the most stressful experience you can go through.[1]

As with anything in life, the stories we hear from others and the statements we read in the press have a lasting impression. When setting out on my very own home sale, I was overwhelmed by the comments and opinions from those around me. For two years prior to putting our home on the market, we had paid our monthly savings into overpaying our mortgage ready to be in the financial position to step up into our next family home. When the day came that we reached our mortgage savings goal, I was over the moon. Saving for two years had been hard work, so to finally get there felt like a dream. Filled with pride, positivity and optimism, I was excited to sell our house and begin the journey towards the dream home for our little, but growing, family.

The day we decided to sell, I told everyone – the cashier at the supermarket, other parents on the school run, family and friends. I was

1 C Canocchi, 'Happy househunting! There's only one thing more stressful than buying a home, finds survey – and that's divorce…', This is Money (8 January 2016), www.thisismoney.co.uk/money/mortgageshome/article-3390039/Only-one-thing-stressful-buying-home-finds-survey-divorce.html, accessed 30 March 2022

so excited. Despite my positivity, the returned message was always the same. Everyone wanted to share their negative home-selling experiences, with few stories of positivity or joy.

In the playground, I heard all about the Clark family having to reduce the price by £20k just to get a viewing. My friends warned me that house prices were sky high and that I would never find a home on my budget. I lost count of the number of times I heard the comment 'rather you than me'. I left every conversation feeling deflated. Within just a few days, the anxiety was building before my property had even gone live on the market.

The excitement that I had been feeling disappeared, and I accepted that selling our home would be stressful. I had absorbed everyone else's stories, warnings and pessimism before having a chance to experience anything for myself.

This is a common occurrence that many home sellers go through. Being surrounded by horror stories, disheartening statistics and negative messages leads them to change their own opinions, casting a shadow on something that should be a truly enlightening experience. Setting off from a position of concern and doubt leads them on a harrowing journey, completely stealing the joy, pride and celebration that they should be enjoying.

Starting your home-selling journey is like starting a new day. Ensuring that you start with a positive mindset and with the best intentions is key. If you have ever woken up not wanting to get out of bed, you'll know exactly what I mean. No one ends a day like that feeling spirited and full of joy; they feel defeated, frustrated. Your home-selling journey is the same. By allowing the scare stories to influence your mindset at the start, you will have already begun a stressful home sale.

One day, while reflecting on my early home-selling experience, I wondered what would happen if we just rubbed out the idea that selling your home is the most stressful experience in your life. What would happen if we no longer gave this notion any credibility? What if we erased the whole sentence from existence and replaced it with thoughts of optimism and positivity? I imagined myself ignoring the stories of the stress and the fearful statistics and blocking out the voices of others around me, replacing them with my own intuition and my reality.

That was the moment that it all became crystal clear. None of the fears that I had been playing out in my mind were real. They had been entirely created from the stories of other people. The false visions of negative property feedback, the fear of not receiving an offer and the pain of our chain falling through was not my story. I had listened so intently to others around me that their experiences had become my own, before they had even happened. It was in my control to stop this, to see possibilities where fear and doubt had been.

My new awareness has driven me to be here with you today, ready to stamp out the stress and bring light to you and the other half-a-million home sellers in the UK each year who, like I was, are affected by the messages of home-selling pressure. With me, selling your home will be purely an experience of moving from one place to the next, on to the latest chapter of your life, no negativity to be found.

Throughout my time in the property industry, my focus has always been on providing an exceptional experience for my clients. There is nothing I love more than being part of my client's journey, listening to them, understanding their reasons for selling and learning their dreams for the future. While my main role as home stager was to prepare and transform their home for a faster sale, I felt myself naturally drawn to provide comfort, support and guidance to improve their selling experience.

Some of the homeowners would be selling for the first time, in a flurry of confusion and anxiety, while others would have already listed their property for sale but be frustrated with the slow progress. Every client had a different back story, but each and every one was stuck in anticipation of a stressful selling process. This resonated so deeply with my own experience, that I began to share elements of my refreshed perspective with them as part of my home-staging service. Rather than purely focusing on furniture placement and colours that enhanced the saleability of their home, I suggested mindful approaches and preparation that brought positive energy to the situation, which previously felt emotionally draining, frustrating or just plain difficult.

The impact was powerful from the outset, with many homeowners finding the shadow of fear lifted away. My guidance and reassurance settled any uneasy thoughts and inspired them to view their endeavours from a new perspective. This was transformational. Feeling supported, they became more empowered to make decisions that better served their property's sale at each step of their selling journey. Not only did this make my clients feel happier, but their new-found positivity seemed to draw in more successful outcomes. All went on to achieve the offer that they had dreamed of within just weeks of us first meeting.

Over the past few years, I have guided hundreds of homeowners through their home-selling journey from preparation to completion, and the rewards of taking my mindful steps have spoken for themselves. From quick kickstart calls to more thorough consultations, the more we connected with the emotion behind the sale process, the greater the success it brought them. Roughly 80% of the homeowners who have reached out to me and taken these steps have achieved their sale within four weeks.

CASE STUDY: STAYING POSITIVE

Susan came to me after being on the market for over a year, having received little interest. She was getting few viewings from the online listing and anyone who came into the property left without making an offer. The general feedback had been vague, so she was feeling lost and unsure of where to turn. Susan no longer lived in the property, as she had moved away to live with her partner. They had been hoping that the sale of the apartment would give them the freedom to buy something together and start a new chapter. This dream moved further away from them the longer the property was on the market, until she eventually lost hope.

At the point of despair, Susan became distanced from it all. She had been so overwhelmed and burnt out with constantly chasing agents and was emotionally drained by let-downs from viewings for the previous year, that she just stopped. She didn't want to call the agents as she feared the outcome of the call. She didn't want to think about the situation at all.

Overcoming Susan's mindset was the most difficult part of her onward selling journey. Reconnecting her with the vision of her new life and supporting her to take back control of her sale transformed her situation. She felt empowered to assess her current agent, took steps to prepare her home to attract the right buyer, and felt excited to relaunch her property on the market. This excitement boosted her communication with the agent, added a spark to her home preparation and gave her a feeling of ease and optimism.

When the launch day came, it was as though the wave of positivity had completely revived her sale. After a morning of viewings, Susan received the call that she had been praying for that year. She had not one, but two offers.

I will never forget answering her that morning. Her tuneful, happy voice told me, 'I've done it. I've got an offer – and I can't believe it!'

She went on to achieve a smooth and stress-free completion.

Susan is just one of many clients who have found that by creating a positive outlook, they were able to make more confident decisions, shape their selling experience and transform the outcome of their sale.

No matter where you are in your selling journey, your sale is within touching distance, and I am here to help. With this book, you will learn how to see your home sale from a completely new perspective and unlock techniques that will catapult your property-selling success. Together, we are going to put an end to feeling powerless, fearful or worried. We'll stamp out any preconceived ideas, any existing fear, anything that isn't supporting your happiness, and give you an experience you will positively reflect upon for years to come.

Your home-selling journey is destined to be full of inspiration, self-reflection and optimism. By understanding that happiness is connected to a successful sale, you can be free of negativity as you move through the sales process. I will guide you through the key stages of your home-selling journey, sharing effective preparation and mindset techniques to support your decisions, success and happiness. These techniques are about to change everything, enrich your perspective and bring joy to your sale.

About the book

In **Chapter 1: Are You Serious?**, I will take you right back to the root of why you are selling your home. This chapter will encourage you to bring self-awareness to your experience and visualise your dream for the future. By the end of this chapter, you will be ready to start (or restart) your journey with passion and focus.

In **Chapter 2: Selecting Your Dream Team**, I give you the confidence to select your dream team, and remind you that this is a decision to purely serve your unique needs. By the end of this chapter, you will be glowing and ready to select the right partners with whom to enjoy this journey.

Chapter 3: Staging To Sell is one of my favourite chapters. Here, I share the tried-and-tested techniques that are guaranteed to capture the loving attention of your future buyer, and allow you to view the sales preparation through a different lens. I show you how inspiring, grounding and fun this stage can be.

In **Chapter 4: Surviving Your Launch**, we look at the marketing stage and create a mindset where you feel empowered and in control. I shall share steps that have transformed the journeys of my clients, keeping them in positive alignment while marketing their property and managing work, home and family life.

It's time to celebrate your offer! **Chapter 5: Celebrate Your Offer** is all about checking in with your emotions and realising the success you have achieved so far. By the end of this chapter, you will have the tools to identify the best offer for you to serve your sale, leaving you more optimistic than ever.

OK, now comes the packing. **Chapter 6: Let's Get Moving** is not only full of hands-on, action-powered advice to get you physically packed, but is here for you on an emotional level as you revisit memories and process the next step of your journey.

Everything you need to transform your home-selling experience is right here in these pages. After all, selling your home will only be whatever you make it. Let's make it happy.

ONE
Are You Serious?

Being sure is so important right now, which is exactly why I wanted Chapter 1 of this book to have such a blunt title. This chapter is going to open everything up, put all your cards on the table and bring you back to your core thinking around your sale. It may feel deep at times, but stay with me, as by connecting with your reasons and your dream for the future, we can make sure you are starting your sales experience in the most powerful way.

You may not be on this journey alone. Your partner, children and siblings may also be key players in this home sale. Knowing you are ready and serious is only the first step when other people are involved. How can you be certain that they are all on the same page as you in their ideas about this sale? Are they truly ready or just following your lead? Together, we'll build greater awareness of not only your vision but also of those around you, to ensure that everyone in your circle is aligned and serious about their role in your home sale. This unity will give you the readiness to move to the next stage.

Why are you selling?

Let's go right back to the starting point of selling your home. When did you first decide to sell? Selling a home is sometimes the most impulsive decision that homeowners make. Scrolling through online property portals one evening or seeing a shift in market values can often trigger conversations about selling up.

The sudden rush of adrenaline and runaway thoughts can quickly lead to spur-of-the-moment estate agent calls. In no time, homeowners can find themselves in a whirlwind of impromptu property viewings and frantic mortgage calculations, all before they have determined whether they are even serious about selling. Making impulsive and spontaneous decisions can feel so exciting, and even unifying when you're sharing the burst of excitement with another. This sudden spark can feel amazing, so it is not surprising to see how the decision to sell up can explode from a non-existent thought to full-blown life event in a matter of moments.

Walking down the high street or searching online, we are surrounded by estate agents and property-selling websites advertising the ability to get you on the market fast, giving homeowners the avenue to react quickly to their knee-jerk decision to sell. Some online property agents even advertise the ability to value your property, place it live online and deliver your 'for sale' board within just five days. Glorifying pacy listings gives the impression that moving quicker to market creates success.

Do not be fooled. Rushing the decision to sell your home is not smart. A hasty decision will immediately put you in a frantic position, leaving you feeling swept along and powerless to the strong current of the sales process. Remember, this is the start of your home-selling journey and beginning from a clear, certain and informed position guarantees you the strongest start to your sale.

If you are reading this and thinking about your snap decision to sell your home, I can completely relate. As a naturally impulsive person myself, I quite often find myself jumping all in on new ideas and dreams. I guess it's the Sagittarian in me! There is no harm in being passion-driven or excited about a new idea. But, let me tell you one thing, being able to guide this energy away from spontaneous action and focus on finding clarity in your decision before taking any steps at all will serve you well.

This was especially real for me in my own home sale back in 2015. At that point, I was six months pregnant and in a real nesting phase. Although we had no plans to sell our home, I often spent time browsing the online listings to see what was available. Most of the time, this was a harmless pastime, but one day I found a house for sale on a pretty cul-de-sac just half a mile from our then home. The 'I need it' reaction was instant and engulfing. I found myself immediately phoning my husband to tell him about the property and arranging estate agents to value our home. Desperation was in the driving seat as I grasped onto the hope that listing our home fast would allow us to make an offer on the impulse house.

Despite not having truly considered whether we could afford to sell, or whether at six months pregnant it was even the right time for us to make the move, we found ourselves in a flurry of activity. After stopping to crunch the numbers, it was clear that we were not ready. It hurt. I could see that it was the truth, but it didn't stop the overwhelming feeling of disappointment. The impulse house was not meant to be.

When I compare this experience to when we actually listed eighteen months later, I cannot believe the difference. Our disappointment encouraged us to stop and talk about what we wanted to achieve when we set out to list our property in the future. For me, I knew that when the time came to sell up for real, I did not want to find myself in that situation again. I wanted to feel clear about what we were aspiring to achieve, confident in our numbers and excited by the journey. The only way that this would happen was to knuckle down ahead of listing and only take action once we were serious about selling our home. No more window-shopping, dreaming or impulsively reacting. It was time to get serious in our decision-making.

It took us eighteen months – eighteen whole months – to be truly ready to list our property on the market. If you are thinking 'I haven't got eighteen months', do not be alarmed. Everyone's situation is different. Some people may need a few months, some a few weeks, some just a few days. The key to it all is making sure that you take time to assess your decision to sell your home before you take any action at all. I mean it! When you jump into action without the full confidence that you are in the right position to sell, you will experience unnecessary anxiety, stress and doubt. I promise you, the time that you spend understanding and bringing clarification to your decisions early in the process will be the best investment you make.

It was, for me, the most powerful turning point in my selling experience. Not only did it set me up on a path to a happy home sale, but it allowed me to discover a powerful decision-making method that has transformed the sales of many homeowners. Every one of my homeowner clients who has followed these steps has left the process happier and clearer about their own situation, going on to achieve a stress-free home sale.

Take as much time as you need to move through these steps. Unlocking the deep and true reasons for your wish to sell your home may not come fast. If you are starting this at the very beginning of your journey, great – you are starting from a clean slate. If you are already on the market, this exercise is even more essential. It will help you understand whether a home sale is indeed the right move for you at this stage. You'll redefine your financial positioning and understand your dream.

For some, the exercise may highlight core issues that they may not have realised were there. It may present deeper emotional or situational pain, such as grief, unhappy relationships or escalating medical problems which cannot be overcome with a home sale. It may prove that the time isn't quite right to sell your home, and that's OK. Do not force your thoughts to fit a decision that isn't right just yet. Embrace the situation that you are in and use the exercise to create alternative options that serve you now and set you up for a sale in the future.

Regardless of where you are in your journey, be ready to regain your confidence. Go deep with your thoughts, play them out in your mind and avoid impulsive, reactive answers. Take time and be patient with yourself. This time is all yours, and it is crucial. You will end this exercise with crystal-clear faith in your selling situation. Whether you are ready today or see the decision to sell as better suited for the future, having this knowledge is transformational. Let's get to it.

EXERCISE: SHOULD I SELL? QUESTIONS TO ASK YOURSELF

Identify the problem

- What is your reason for wanting to sell your home?
- What is it about your current home that is not suitable?
- What do you need that your current home doesn't offer?

Get the facts

- What are the features you need in a home to enable you to live your happiest life?
- Is there a specific price point, location or size that makes this possible?
- What does this look like financially?

- How much do properties like this cost in the area you need?

Know what you can afford

- Have you completed an affordability calculator or spoken to a mortgage advisor?
- What will the cost be to move home?

Brainstorm alternative solutions

- Are there any reasons why you shouldn't sell right now?
- Is there another way to achieve what you want without moving home?
- Can you solve your problem without moving?
- Is the grass really greener?
- What would your alternative option(s) cost?
- What would they look like?
- Would they solve the problem?
- Will that option achieve what you hope to achieve?
- How does that feel?

By considering all your options, you will be able to identify whether you need to move or whether holding back on a sale is going to better serve you at this time. Regardless of the outcome, with the knowledge you have gained, you have just given yourself the best start to your happy home sale, whenever it may be.

Seller's remorse

All too often, I meet clients who have powered through the selling process without considering their reasons or exploring their options. Needless to say, it delivers a panic-fuelled, stressful sale, often ending in seller's remorse.

Seller's remorse happens when a homeowner realises that they no longer want to sell their home after they have listed on the market. This could be for a number of reasons, which could have been addressed earlier if they had sufficiently considered their decision ahead of placing their property on the market.

CASE STUDY: CONSIDERING ALL OPTIONS

This couldn't have been truer than in the selling story of one of my loveliest clients, Mrs Jennings, who placed her family home on the market after losing her job. This was not something that she had anticipated, and being on the market broke her heart. Working with homeowners, I have experienced every wave of emotion, from heartache to elation, but Mrs Jennings' emotions were deep. Her devastation, disappointment and remorse were the worst I had ever experienced.

Mrs Jennings reached out to me as she was struggling to sell her home and was not achieving the offers that she had expected. But our meeting uncovered much more than the basic home-staging support that she thought she needed. We spoke for hours about her home and the reason she was selling. She shared stories about her perfect home, its beautiful location and reminisced about walking her children to school through the wooden garden gate. She was now struggling to keep up with the running costs, with her job having ended so abruptly.

As she spoke about her home, she smiled, but her eyes looked sad. She told me that she had put her property on the market the moment she lost her job, to protect her family from financial hardship. It was the only solution she could think of.

Her knee-jerk reaction was a clear defence mechanism, blocking the pain of her job loss and taking action that distracted her from the root cause of this pain. She wanted to feel in control, but was in fact feeling more and more out of control than before. She was immediately thrown into seeing every available property and desperately booking viewings in the hope that an offer would relieve her stress and pain. The panic and overwhelm blocked her from making decisions or preparing her home to sell, because, behind the impulsive fiery feeling of needing to sell, she just didn't want to.

The turning point for Mrs Jennings came with one simple question: 'Do you really need to sell?'

After a moment, she began to come up with solutions that could help her to get into a better position without selling her beloved home. It was that simple. Just by stopping to ask the question and reflect on alternative solutions, she was able to see exactly what she wanted to do and take happier steps to explore them.

Just a few months later, Mrs Jennings called. The sadness had been replaced with a joyful confidence. She had continued to explore other options to create the happy life she wanted while continuing to live in

> her home. The power of pausing to think about her situation from a position of clarity was the greatest step she had taken.

Gaining clarity about your situation and understanding whether selling your home is your perfect ending will give you the power to get serious about your next steps. When you know for sure that selling your home is what you want, you will step into the process with confidence. Combine this confidence with vision, and you'll bring everything together.

What's your vision?

Your goal may be to sell up to live with a new partner, to move into your next family home, say goodbye to a lost loved one or create a happier future. Every sale has its own story and everyone that I meet has a different vision.

Focusing on your end goal brings everything closer. No matter what I have been doing in life – whether selling a home, starting my business or even writing this book – having my vision clear in the forefront of my mind has kept me on the right path. It's much easier to make the right decision or choose the right path when you know exactly where you want to end up.

Creating your vision is the best exercise. Now that you are confident in your selling situation, you can let your imagination run away with itself. Use of visualisation techniques to manifest goals has become a more prominent practice in helping people realise their full potential in other areas of their lives. It's the same when applied to a home-selling journey. The focus, clarity and positive mindset that you'll create through visualising your destination will not only guide you to achieve your vision but will also help you keep it a calm and joyful experience.

EXERCISE: FIVE-MINUTE VISUALISATION

Take a moment to close your eyes and imagine yourself standing in front of a door. This is the front door to your next chapter, the front door to your new home and new life.

Now imagine turning the handle. Really feel in your hand the metal of the door handle as you firmly press it down or twist it. This is the first time that you have entered, and a wave of achievement, relief and comfort waves across you. You feel it move through your fingertips, travel up your arms and through your body. Revived and renewed energy is present and brings light throughout your body.

Take a moment to feel this and connect with this moment that you begin your new chapter.

Knowing where you want to be is the firmest foundation you can give yourself for this process. Visualisation helps you define where you want to be so that you can move towards your new chapter in a way that feels effortless, familiar and certain. This confidence will see you take the right steps and decisions to achieve exactly what you need, when you need it.

For some, physical visualisation techniques can have more impact. This may involve printing off a photo of your family in a location or carrying an extra key fob on your chain for your new home. Connecting with a physical image or symbol representing your visions is a joyful reminder of where you are heading. For others, visualisation can be more inward. If this is you, take time daily (while enjoying your coffee, for example) to imagine yourself in the midst of your dream life having achieved your home sale.

It is amazing how uplifting it can feel when stepping into the vision of the day you receive your offer, opening the door to your new property or closing the door on a past experience. Seeing yourself in the story triggers the feelings and emotions connected to the real moment, creating a powerful shift from helplessly trying to sell your home to feeling as though you are already achieving it. With this positive and focused mindset, there will be no room for any of the common home-selling fears, anxieties or stresses. Positive visions give you the power, strength and path to create your happy home-selling experience.

Who's with you?

Selling your home is rarely a solo decision, with immediate family members, friends or distant relatives having a financial or emotional investment in the outcome. Handling others' expectations can bring overwhelming challenges throughout the home-selling process, but together, we can overcome that. I have experienced everything from unruly teens who refuse to get out of bed for viewings to elderly siblings who just can't agree on a sale price. No matter the situation, one thing is always true. Their frustration is not because of the home sale itself but because of a misalignment in communication and vision.

When placing a property on the market, consideration of the other people affected by the sale can come as an afterthought. We often treat one home as a single entity, assuming that every person has the same expectation. This couldn't be any further from the truth. A situation that may seem matter of fact to one family member may bring emotional turmoil to another. It is incredible how different each individual's perspective can be in one household alone. Sellers can find themselves confused and frustrated by their family members or friends, especially if they do not take time in the early stages of the process to understand their different positions.

All parties involved in a property sale need to be on the same page as you are. This sounds self-explanatory, but it is frequently not the case. Have you spoken to your family? Parents regularly make decisions without their children's input and adult siblings take action without one another's consent, leading to complications further down the line.

Stop. Take a moment to pause, step away from your own thoughts, your own visions, and your own reason to sell, and consider the others first. Consider whether you have taken the time to ensure that the people in your home or involved in your sale have the same expectations as you.

It is incredibly important to remember that your connection with your home may not be the same as theirs. For children, a family home may be the only home they have ever known. After a bereavement or divorce, a beloved home may hold uncomfortable or painful memories for some but have less emotional charge for others.

Each individual is different, and understanding the position of each party in your sale is going to help you create a journey to best serve you all. After all, when you all take steps in the same direction, you will achieve the outcome you want in a smoother, faster and happier way. You may be streets ahead of them in your mindset, having already spent time assessing your decision to sell and understanding your vision. Your patience, understanding and lead in encouraging these steps for others is so important.

Take time to speak to every individual about the home sale and identify whether they even want to sell. Encourage them to understand why they want to sell, what the home means to them and what their vision for the future is. Likewise, sharing your thoughts, decisions and vision for your home-selling journey will allow them to understand your position in the process.

Not every family or situation will be filled with love and friendship – for some, this may be the most difficult step of the entire selling process. But creating a united front to achieve a goal is essential, so be clear and show that you are ready to work with others to achieve your sale. This may not always be a comfortable conversation to have, especially if your sale involves dispute, divorce or probate, but working together to achieve your sale will allow all involved to move on to their next chapter, whatever that may be.

CASE STUDY: SIBLING DISAGREEMENT IN A PROBATE SALE

The above couldn't have been any truer than with the Hopkin family. With three siblings – George, Barbara and Cathy – holding financial and emotional interest in their late father's home, the home-selling process was a mess. With probate now complete and each sibling having equal ownership in the property, they needed to find a solution that would serve them all. However, each sibling had different expectations of the sale. George wanted to get the sale completed as soon as possible. He very much viewed the property as bricks and mortar. It was the place his father had lived, but there was no emotional link for him between his father and the property. He was heavily involved in the sale process and was the key player in speaking to external parties. Barbara was living overseas and also wanted a quick property sale. While she was not interested in being involved in the day-to-day process, she was focused on spend. She wanted a low-rate agent, low-ball solicitors and minimal investment in the sale. Cathy was in a different position. She had lived with her father in the years leading to his passing, so was deeply connected to the property. For her, the property was her last remaining link to her father.

Each of the sibling's desires to sell and individual visions were so different that all three of them were pulling the sale in different directions, adding a mountain of unnecessary stress to what had already been a painful twelve-month probate period. The property sat unsold for an additional nine months. An impulsively selected budget agent failed to effectively market the property, and even when viewings took place, it was either shown to non-suitable prospective buyers or was so ill-prepared for viewings that people walked away. It was frustrating, and this feeling only escalated as the siblings became increasingly irritated with the actions and reactions of the others.

When I met them, the tension was palpable. George was so keen to sell, he wanted to explore the idea of fully dressing and staging the property to boost its appeal and relaunch on the market. Barbara was sceptical and didn't want to spend any money to prepare the place, and Cathy looked lost. It was clear that the issues that they were facing with their sale were not related to the property at all, but the mindset of the siblings and the environment that this created.

While their situation felt like a mess, it was straightforward to resolve. By having the opportunity to talk through their selling situation with an outsider – in this case, me – they began to see their situation from a new perspective. This simple yet effective level of communication had been left unaddressed in the early stages, so it became buried and ignored. Now, out in the open, the family could understand and appreciate one another's views. We were able to continue through to a successful sale.

I will share the steps we took to create their happy home sale over the next few chapters.

A great way to break the ice when discussing the possible sale of a property is to openly engage any family, friends and other parties interested in your sale in the process. You may like to do this with a few conversation prompt cards over dinner, a questionnaire on email or something a little more formal. Depending on your situation, some setups may suit you better. But whatever option you choose, taking time to unite everyone and identify their expectations as part of the early decision-making process will set you off on the right foot.

The power of unity and alignment will help you achieve the happy home sale that you deserve. Having seen first-hand the amazing results that my clients have achieved by opening up to others involved in their sale, I implore you to make this a key step before starting your home-selling journey. From chatting with young children over a special breakfast to having tough emotional conversations with elderly family members, open and honest communication brings people together and reduces uncertainty or frustration.

EXERCISE: CONVERSATION STARTERS

Here are some key prompts to help you get started in building these conversations with others. Adjust them as you need to for different parties, eg, children, siblings, parents.

- What are your immediate thoughts about selling the home?
- What memories or feelings does this sale trigger?
- What will your situation be if the home is sold?
- Where will you live or stay if the property is sold?
- Is this your ideal situation?
- What is your vision or dream?

- How can this sale support you achieving what you hope to achieve?
- Does your financial position tally with your goal?
- How do you want to be involved in the sale?
- How can we work together to create a stress-free and happy sale?

Check out my web page natalieevansuk.com to get your hands on free downloadable conversation cards and family questionnaires to help you navigate these conversations in a fun and refreshing way. Remember the more joy you bring to the process, the more joy you will attract.

Home-selling Myth 1: Selling your home will solve all problems

For some, selling a home may be the key to achieve their dreams. For others, the decision may be a reaction or distraction from a greater emotional or situational problem. Not everyone is ready to begin a home-selling journey the moment that they need or want to do so, and that's OK. What's important is being able to identify this before you start powering through the selling journey.

Summary

In this chapter, we stripped everything back to look at the reasons behind your decision to sell, so that you can make an informed decision from a clear and impulse-free mindset as to whether you are serious about selling. This is a powerful position to be in, and you should feel lighter just knowing you are committed and in a strong position to achieve your vision. Fixing your dream for your future life in your thoughts in a daily visualisation practice will keep you moving on the right path.

We looked at the setup of your sale and considered the other key players who may have a stake in the outcome. From siblings to housemates, anyone who is involved in your sale will need to be in alignment with your vision for the process to run smoothly. Together, we have considered ways that we can understand the mindset of others involved in your sale and learnt to be empathetic to their situation. Their vision may not be the same as yours, but with a unified approach to the home-selling journey, you can all in turn achieve what you desire. Better still, you will achieve it in a happier way.

TWO

Selecting Your Dream Team

Just saying 'dream team' fills me with the feeling of encouragement and support, and this is exactly how I want you to feel as we enter this part of the journey. In this chapter, we are going to look at the people who will surround, serve and support you throughout your home sale. By understanding who you need, why you need them and how to select the person for you, you'll be ready to find the key partners who will make your dream a reality. Better still, by surrounding yourself with the right team, you will feel respected and empowered to get the happy home sale that you deserve.

By the end of this chapter, you will feel confident to make decisions that will serve you. It is going to feel transformational – there'll be less worry, less chasing, less doubt. You will have peace of mind that your dream team is working for you, with your vision in mind.

The emphasis is on *your* dream team. Selecting people whose input in your home-selling journey centres on you is essential. This doesn't mean ignoring their advice or recommendations, but it does mean putting your needs at the heart of the process and making sure that you consider their guidance in relation to your situation.

As with any purchase, it is natural to reach out to others for their advice. In fact, over half of UK consumers use word-of-mouth recommendations to select products and services over branding and reviews.[2] But, remember this, the recommendation made to you by another person will be based on the service that they needed. The same goes for your dream team. While you may trust their opinion and

2 'Consumer trust in online, social and mobile advertising grows', Nielsen (March 2012), www.nielsen.com/us/en/insights/article/2012/consumer-trust-in-online-social-and-mobile-advertising-grows, accessed 30 March 2022

know wholeheartedly that they support your sale, they will base their guidance on their home-selling experience, not yours. What has worked for them may not work for you. Recommendations can be a great source of information when you assess them objectively. But remember that your choices are your own. You do not need to feel pressured into following the advice of others.

Remember this:

- Every seller is different – their need for support, their demographic, their personality and their communication style vary.
- Every property is different – their styling, layout, location and history are unique.
- Every single home sale is different – the reasons for sale, the time frame, the key players are individual to that situation.

If you do receive recommendations, greet them from a place of gratitude and confidence. Thank your friend for sharing and tell them that you will be having a look at several options to create the best decision for your sale. Feel confident in the preparation you have already done in understanding your reasons for selling and your end vision, and know that you are ready to find the best partners for your dream team.

Key players in the home-selling process

Let's take a brief look at the key players who you'll need in your dream team and the role they'll play.

Financial advisor: A financial advisor is a professional who reviews your personal finances and advises on your situation.

Mortgage broker: Your mortgage broker reviews your current financial situation and confirms your property affordability based on your income and outgoings.

While a broker may not advise you on your personal finances, they will find a selection of mortgage products for you from their panel of lenders. They often have access to better rates than external mortgage applicants. They have expert knowledge in lending and are a great support throughout the process.

Mortgage lender: The mortgage lender is the bank or building society that lends the funds for a property purchase.

Estate agent: The estate agent is the key player in marketing and securing a sale on your property, or your onward purchase. They handle communication between all members of your dream team to ensure the sale progresses smoothly.

Home stager: A home stager is an expert in ensuring that a property is presented in the best way to go on the market. They provide a range of support, from consultation services and gentle preparation to fully furnishing empty homes.

EPC assessor: When placing your home on the market, you are legally required to have a valid Energy Performance Certificate (EPC). An EPC assessor will evaluate a property to give it a rating.

Solicitor (conveyancer): The solicitor (or conveyancer) manages the legal process of transferring a property from one owner to another. They validate funds, check property details by raising searches, and draw legal contracts for the sale.

Mortgage valuer: The mortgage valuer confirms a property's value. For your onward purchase, your mortgage lender may arrange for a valuation to be carried out at your prospective property before they agree to lend the mortgage. For your property sale, your buyer's mortgage company will book a suitable time for their mortgage valuer to visit.

Surveyor: A surveyor reviews your prospective property and carries out a detailed inspection of the property's condition. You will need to arrange this for your onward home. For your sale, your buyer will arrange for their surveyor to visit your home.

Mover: A mover or removal supplier takes your furniture and belongings from one location to another. This may be to your next home or to another location, such as a storage facility.

Selling your home is a full team effort, and knowing who you need in your dream team is just the start. Applying your self-awareness and crystal-clear knowledge of your selling situation when selecting your dream team is where the magic happens. Knowing what to look for and how to see if your agent, solicitor or surveyor is the right fit for you will help you to avoid the frustrating traps that homeowners fall into – or feel forced into – when selling their home.

The price trap

The biggest trap that I see is price. People are pulled towards a service because of its low rates and reduced fees. We are in a culture where getting value is interpreted as getting value for money, ie, the cheapest possible price. This approach is flawed when choosing the right people to lead your home sale. Don't get me wrong, not all lower-fee agents or suppliers will lead to heartache, but trust me when I say in many cases, you get what you pay for. It is essential when reviewing your dream team selections that you consider the value as being much more than purely monetary.

Each key player listed above is integral to your journey. Their expertise, communication skills and motivation will see you achieve your home sale. Having total, unquestionable confidence in your dream team's ability to own their part of the process will reduce any pressure on you during this exciting time. Let me ask you one thing – is it worth cutting corners and favouring cheaper rates over ability and engagement?

Time and time again, I meet homeowners who have been left disappointed by the service that they received from their chosen agents, solicitors and financial partners. Why? Because they went with the cheaper option. Over time, this decision brought all manner of pain and frustration to their selling experience. Stories of lapsed communication, lack of proactivity, reduced property exposure and failed sales all highlight the importance of stepping away from a money mindset and towards one based on competence.

Now is the time to push aside any drive towards getting a bargain during your home sale and focus on the factors that will create the happiest selling experience. Your intuition is powerful. Trusting this and evaluating the immediate connection you have with each of your potential dream team partners will bring so much light to your journey. Combining this connection with confidence in their expertise will give you the greatest peace of mind that everything will align seamlessly for you to achieve your vision.

Evaluating your dream team

Let's look at some key considerations for selecting the right dream team member for you. Shake off that 'spend less' mindset and focus on your connection with the individual and your awareness of their expertise. From estate agents to home-staging support, these are great starting points to help you make the right choice, first time:

- Before taking any further steps, be sure to understand exactly who your contact will be, and speak to that person. Just because Julie on reception makes you feel amazing, doesn't mean that Jennie will. **Speak to your contact.**
- From the moment you speak, do you feel **respected**? Has the individual called you back on time, as scheduled? Have they provided you with the information that you were expecting, in the time frame agreed?

- Is there clear **two-way communication** between you and the individual or does it feel one-sided, like a sales pitch?
- Does the individual listen with **genuine understanding and interest** as you share your expectations and onward vision? Do they reference things that you have said within their own communication? Do they seem excited to work with you, asking questions about you and your situation?
- Take a moment to **think about how you feel** when speaking to the individual for the first time. It is normal to feel a little nervous, but does this ease as the conversation progresses? The right dream team player will ensure you feel completely comfortable, in control and at ease.
- Every professional has a specialism, even if they do not realise it. **Does their specialism match your situation?** Refer back to the dream team list to get a better idea of what this may mean for each individual.
- For some dream team members, **experience in your property's location**

will give them stronger client databases, greater locational knowledge and geographical resources to help your sale progress smoothly. This is especially true for estate agents and surveyors.

- Check out former clients' reviews. Does this person have the **credentials**, the professional experience and success stories behind them to back up their expertise?
- Does this individual feel **authentic** in their wish to support you to achieve your sale and onward vision?
- **If at any point you feel uncomfortable, inferior, or distrust the individual, they are not the person for you. Walk away.**

Shop around and speak to several professionals on your quest to find your dream team. You may not find the right person the first time, and that's OK. It's better than OK, actually. You should feel proud that you are so aligned with your expectations and vision that you know exactly what you are hoping to get from your dream team. Such self-awareness will mean that the moment you feel someone is right, you'll know.

There should be no pressure when choosing your dream team, so take your time and trust your instincts. After all, these are the people who will support you through your journey.

CASE STUDY: THE POWERHOUSE AGENT

I'll never forget my first estate agent experience. Reflecting back on it today, I wish I'd had the knowledge that I am sharing with you right now, because I could not have got my decision more wrong.

Sitting in my living room, I met three local estate agents. The first just seemed to talk at me, making no eye contact. Needless to say he was a straight-up no. The second was nice – a guy called Sam. Sam talked through our sale and vision and understood what we wanted to achieve. He explained that he would be our first point of contact throughout the process as well as being the person on site for all viewings. His supportive nature and genuine interest in our home felt reassuring and gave us immediate trust in his experience and belief in his interest in our sale.

Then came the curveball. The third agent was a total powerhouse. Smartly dressed and confident, he arrived in his sports car, with impressive digital brochures and effortlessly highlighted statistics on local sales and his success rates in our area. He knew his stuff and had the total wow factor. We were blown away by his unquestionable confidence and had every belief that with that much power behind it, our house would sell in a snap.

The experience that we had with the two agents couldn't have been more different. With one, we felt trusting and reassured, yet with the other, we felt impressed with the power and ego. We were so torn.

My initial feeling was to go all in on the powerhouse, but something was tugging at me to give Sam a shot. We decided to instruct both agents on dual agency. This was still the wrong decision. You'll see why.

When I called both agents, the responses were polar opposite. From Sam, the response was welcoming and continued to reflect the relationship that we had already begun to build. He was thankful, excited to be instructed and ready to go. His energy and drive were clear and immediately made me feel reassured.

But the powerhouse crushed us. The bold, confident voice that had presented

> successful statistics was full of arrogance and anger, dismissing the idea of dual agency and putting our choice down. He made us feel stupid, talking about how we were preventing our home from selling because of our terrible decision. I felt completely overpowered and inferior.
>
> It is never OK for someone to make you feel this way, and I should have walked away then. I didn't.

I, like many homeowners, fell into the trap of believing that powerful voices, shiny shoes and confident pitches would create the best home-selling partner, when in reality, this led to frustration. If you feel anything other than listened to and understood by a property professional, they are not the right person for you. It is never OK to feel disrespected or belittled. If this happens to you, have the self-respect and confidence to walk away. I wish I had.

I always remind my clients of one thing. Each member of your dream team has a key role in making sure that your property sale progresses smoothly. But central to it all is you. You are the most important person in this journey. You need to be sure that aside from the work that your dream team are doing and the professional expertise they are bringing to your sale, you have people working with you who want to see you succeed, who are excited to be part of your journey, and who see you as a valued part of the process. You need to like them and they need to like you, because without this foundation, you will lose your connection, your trust and your confidence.

At this early stage of your home-selling journey, you hold all the power. This is your time to push aside any beliefs you have about unhelpful estate agents or non-communicative solicitors and find professionals who dispel these myths. Sculpt a dream team who gives you the support, guidance and professional expertise that you need to achieve your vision. There is no better feeling at the start of your journey than knowing that you are surrounded by people who you have faith in, and who in turn make you feel respected and valued.

Choose your team wisely

Most professionals will tell you that they are the right person for the job. Which is why when you are looking for your perfect estate agent or best-suited solicitor, you need to enter conversations with absolute clarity on what you need. Have the confidence to push for the information that will enable you to make the best decision.

One of the biggest frustrations of my homeowner clients is that they find themselves trapped, listed with the wrong agent for weeks, reducing their price to desperately draw attention to their property, only to discover that it was the agent who was a poor match in the first place. Properties that sit on the market for extended periods lose significant appeal, so by wasting time with the wrong agent and spending longer on the market, you will see interest drop, resulting in low-ball offers, if any at all. By taking the effort to select the right person, you'll create a much happier home-selling experience and save yourself time and money in the long run.

This frustration recently presented itself to me when my grandfather placed his home on the market. By recently, I mean right now. Literally while editing this chapter, I received a call from my mother to say that after losing his wife only a few months ago, my grandfather had made the emotional decision to sell his three-bedroom family home. He had lived in the property for over fifty years, but had decided to start a new chapter and find a development offering better living facilities for a gentleman of his wise age. Of course, I asked 101 questions and wanted to fully unpick and understand the actions he had taken and where he was in the process.

Fiercely independent, he had found his new home, put in an offer *and* signed an agreement with the same estate agent within just a few days. You may be wondering, 'Why is that so wrong?' It's fast, but it sounds efficient, right?

Wrong. My grandfather had not bought or sold a property for years. He hadn't set foot inside an estate agency, and certainly was not up to speed with the world of online property portals and social media. Unknown to him, he had fallen into the trap of impulsively going with the first estate agent he contacted. Let me ask you this – is the high-street agent with a window full of retirement properties really going to be the best option for the sale of a three-bedroom family property?

We will look at your buyer in much more detail in the next chapter, but for now, just know that every single property has a different target buyer demographic, for example: family, first-time buyer, downsizer, etc. In the case of my grandfather's three-bedroom family home, it is highly likely that the best-suited target buyer is a young family.

Every buyer demographic will look for homes in different ways. Older buyers may prefer a traditional high-street agent with plenty of face-to-face contact, whereas a first-time buyer in their late twenties may spot their dream home through social media platforms such as Instagram.

Making sure that your chosen agent has access to buyers fitting your target buyer demographic is essential. If they have a database full of the wrong clients or if they focus on the wrong marketing technique, you can guarantee a prolonged and painful sale.

Home-selling Myth 2: Surveyors, agents and brokers are all the same

It is so wild to think that most of the time, we assume that every surveyor, estate agent, conveyancer, home stager or mortgage broker does the same job, when in other areas of our life, we buy cars from dealers who specialise in our brand of choice, we visit specialist retailers for different services and know that business competitors have different target clients.

Every professional in the property industry has their circle of expertise and a preferred client. This may be based on property location, value or status. When you understand your situation, your needs and your expectations, you will be ready to find the professional who best serves you – the professional who deserves a spot in your dream team.

Summary

In this chapter, we have looked at the roles that property professionals play in your home-selling journey, and the key players you'll need in your dream team. You have come to understand how important you are in this selection process and know the considerations to keep in mind when selecting professionals. In short, base your choices on connection and expertise over money and power. It is essential that your dream team works effectively in pursuit of the sale that you need to move on to your next chapter. By surrounding yourself with a trusted dream team who communicate respectfully and understand your vision, you will be on the road to achieving the smooth and happy home sale you deserve.

THREE

Staging To Sell

Now that you've got your dream team selected, you're ready to get your property listed, right? No! Hold still for one moment, because things are about to get transformational. It's one thing when a potential buyer makes an offer on your home; it's a total game changer when your dream buyer gives you what you want and more. With a little preparation, you can have this.

This chapter is all about giving you the tools to achieve mind-blowing results by being smart about property preparation. I'll shine a light on how your emotional attachment to your property may be holding you back and share ways to move past this to present your home for maximum market appeal. We'll step out of your shoes and into those of your dream buyer. We'll make sure that your property is capturing their attention from the moment they stroll – or scroll – past it.

Property preparation and staging is my super-power and I am so ready to be part of this journey with you. Let me say one thing before I go all in on this: I am so proud of you right now. I know we are still at this early stage of your selling journey, but you are doing amazingly. The early stages of your happy home-selling journey require a lot of deep work and thinking that many do not tackle so soon, if at all. But you are taking time to build awareness of your selling situation, align your visions and prepare your dream team, putting you miles ahead in your journey.

There is one final piece to the puzzle before you launch your home on the market, and that is making sure that your home is ready. Think of your home's online listing as being like any product advertisement. You want to make sure that it not only looks great but captures the attention you want, from the person you want.

This is exactly what we are going to work through together.

Home preparation – where to start?

The idea of sorting, organising, decluttering and going back and forth on the dreaded tip runs can feel overwhelming at the best of times. Perhaps that is why so many homeowners leave this late into their selling process or (foolishly) skip it entirely. Trust me when I say that taking time to understand who you are selling to, knowing how to capture their attention, and creating the space for them to visualise their life in your home will give you the greatest feeling of liberation and power.

Boosting the appeal of your home can have a mind-blowing impact. The smallest alteration can see your home sell faster and even achieve over your anticipated asking price. You simply need to know what steps to take, and, importantly, to take action. That's right. As much as I am a deep believer in positive mindset and the power of manifestation, I have yet to see a property transform itself with no human input.

If that feels too difficult, there is a whole industry of home-staging professionals out there ready to support you through this process. I'll tell you more about how to find them later. Just by understanding the power of careful preparation and home staging, you are already on to a winner.

A word of warning: be ready to become the talk of the town. Your friends will be intrigued to know how you are managing to achieve so much in such a short period of time. Every client I work with is so excited by the results of their preparation and the impact it has on their sale. They are always messaging to say that they feel like preparation preachers to family and friends. You will be no different.

Begin with your buyer

We chuck our properties on the market with minimal effort before listing, hoping that someone will see through the current story it is telling and visualise their own future. Let's erase this idea right away. Buyers are unable to visualise their future in a property when they are forced to see the story of someone else's life. When buying a property, buyers are not just investing in bricks and mortar but in their new, aspirational future lifestyle.

Understanding what drives your dream buyer and adjusting the appearance and ambience of your home to connect with them is crucial. Every single property that goes on the market, including yours, should be thoughtfully considered before anyone snaps their marketing images or conducts viewings. Even the most immaculate, picture-perfect homes benefit from home-staging alterations to make sure that they tick all the right boxes for their dream buyers.

Take a moment to scroll through Rightmove. You will be overwhelmed by the number of homes that have just been thrown on the market with no prior thought. Unmade beds, clothes airers, underwear on the radiators – you'll see it all. Now ask yourself, what does that tell you about that home? Would you be comfortable investing your future life there? Do you want your home to be marketed in this way?

On the flip side, you will also see the most beautiful homes not selling as fast as you would expect. Regardless of whether your home is sparkling or tired, there is always a need to make sure that it is effectively prepared to sell. This doesn't necessarily mean painting, decluttering or spending thousands on refurbishing, but it does mean taking time to think deeply about the message that your home is sending.

I implore you to have an open mind when I tell you this, and remember that I am guiding you from a place of love and support. OK, here goes. It's not all about you anymore. It's time to take yourself out of the centre of this story, and focus all your attention on one person: your dream buyer.

Picture the scene. Your dream buyer is scrolling online day and night for their new home. They know their vision and have a list of everything that they want from their next property. As they pass by the endless ill-prepared houses, they begin to feel frustrated and disheartened. Until… *Pow!* There it is, the home – your home – that immediately draws them in and ticks all the boxes. It is as though it has been posted just for them! That is the power of home staging and effective preparation.

Tackle your emotions

You have the power to achieve this. But first, you'll need to take yourself out of the story and disconnect emotionally from your property. Whether you are selling your own home or the home of a loved one, taking a moment to reminisce and acknowledge the end of this chapter of your life is essential. You'll create the mental space to find the focus you need on the job at hand – preparing your home to sell, so that you can move on to your next chapter.

Many people become protective and hold on to their home and memories with a tight grip. But by being too connected to the property as *your* home will restrict your ability to visualise how it needs to be perceived to attract your dream buyer.

Seeing your property as someone else's home has to be one of the hardest mental milestones to achieve. My clients often describe this as the most difficult part of their home-selling journey, and they're not wrong. But it is also the most rewarding. Every room in your home, each item of furniture, soft toy or ornament holds a story and a memory – some wonderful, some triggering. There is always a fear that by moving on emotionally, you will cause all the memories to be forgotten. Never.

The bricks, timbers, and 'things' in your home do not define or own the memories. The memories are yours forever, and you'll take them with you to your new chapter. Taking this step right now guarantees you'll get there quicker.

There is so much comfort and safety held in the things that we own. But to a buyer who has no personal association with the items, they can tell a vivid story about life in the home and this story may not align with their vision. Sometimes it can make them walk away.

Prospective buyers are not viewing a property for the windows and doors; they are seeking a new and aspirational life. They may be seeking their dream home, their retirement nest or their first step on the property ladder, and each buyer type has a different expectation. An up-levelling house hunter may be seeking an enviable Instagram-worthy life. A retirement-nest seeker may be looking for a calm haven. A first-time buyer may want to see a home that they can grow into with time. Giving each buyer the opportunity to visualise the lifestyle they want is key. After all they might not like the same things as you, and that's OK. You don't want to be their friend – you want them to buy your home.

CASE STUDY: ALIGNING YOUR PROPERTY WITH YOUR DREAM BUYER

Jane was navigating a difficult divorce with her husband. After separating, they had decided to still cohabit, as their home was large enough to offer them the space that they needed while selling and seeking new homes. During this period, the home sat on the market for over a year, and viewer after viewer walked away. While in an aspirational location, with other homes in the area flying off the market, they could not secure an offer.

Agents could not understand why the property was failing to sell, and even price reductions couldn't solve the problem. But on visiting the home, it was clear for me to see – or rather, feel.

Let me tell you a little bit about the human brain. Deep within the brain, there is a group of interconnected structures called the limbic system. These structures play a part in driving our emotional and behavioural reactions, including the powerful 'love at first sight' sensation, when you fall head over heels but you can't explain the rationale behind the feeling.

The same applies when buyers are viewing a home. They have an incredible innate ability to sense when something just doesn't feel right. Hello, limbic system.

This is exactly why Jane's home was not getting the reaction that it should have been. While it was a beautiful home, the physical separation of husband and wife across the house was strong enough to plant the subconscious feelings of disruption, sadness and confusion in the people viewing it. This was not the lifestyle that buyers wanted for their next home. They therefore left the property feeling that it 'wasn't for them', but were not able to constructively pinpoint the fault.

Though my observation about this was completely different from any other advice that she had received, the concept made sense to Jane. She was determined to make the changes she needed to get her offer and achieve the onward peace she was dreaming of. Together, we created an action plan to prepare the property to present the story that her target buyer was looking for. We made gentle changes to reduce the feeling of separation and boost the sense of unity and love.

This transformed the property's sale. Jane received two offers just twenty-four hours after staging her home. By taking a step out of her situation and viewing the property from the perspective of her dream buyer, she revived her sale and stepped closer to her new life.

Decorate for your buyer, not for yourself

Recently, I was speaking to an older man in the supermarket. He had seen my van and asked me about home staging. He said that he was at his wit's end, having spent weeks refreshing every room in his house, even buying new cushions to finish the rooms, but despite his efforts, he still had no offer. He described his home with great admiration and said that he loved his large bookcases, deep red living room wall and was especially proud to have found cushions to match. I told the man that it was amazing that he was putting so much effort into preparing his home and that his hard work deserves an offer, but I offered up one piece of advice.

I often hear these tales of homeowners going all out painting rooms, buying new accessories and refreshing their home to sell, but still finding themselves in a quandary without the result they were hoping for. Why? Because they did the work and prepared the property without knowing who they were selling it to. The paint colours, the cushions, the accessories – they selected them all based on their personal choices and not the items that would capture the attention of their dream buyer. The gentleman was thinking about his home from his point of view, not the point of view of his dream buyer, who was, in fact, thirty years his junior.

The way that we enjoy our homes and the way that they need to be presented for the perfect sale are two different things. Do not rush into making alterations without understanding who you're doing this for.

EXERCISE: UNDERSTANDING YOUR BUYER

Grab a notebook and pen and answer the following questions:

1. Who is going to buy your home?
2. What are the key things that they will be looking for in a home?
3. What do they need in a property?
4. What features in your home align with their needs?
5. What features in your home challenge their needs?

Getting to grips with your buyer's needs like this will allow you to put things right in your property before you spend time and effort preparing your home for the wrong target audience.

Identifying your buyer profile

When I meet clients, they are always blown away by what I am about to tell you, not because it is off-the-chart revolutionary, but because they simply never considered it. It is a hard and fast way to immediately pinpoint who your buyer will be, and 99% of the time it is correct. Ready?

The person who is going to buy your home is likely to be in the same stage of life as you were when you bought it.

Take a moment to think back to when you first started looking for your current home. Whether that was five, ten, fifteen or even thirty years ago, so much changes in life that the needs, wants and desires of your dream buyer will be different from yours today. Tap in to you as you were back then.

Were you starting out on the market? Retiring? Starting a family? Relocating for a city career? Your story then is likely to be their story now, so being aware of where you were and what you were doing will give you a firm grounding for identifying who they are.

Times are changing and the needs of people in certain age categories may differ from what they were for a person of that age a decade ago. Perhaps your target buyer doesn't fit the above rule, but don't worry – in that case, we can look at three simple things:

1. **Recent buyer profile:** The life-cycle of a community is ever evolving. Look at recent

buyers in the area to give you an idea of who your buyer might be.

2. **Professional advice:** Seek advice from local estate agents, home-staging professionals and online sources, such as Zoopla and the UK Office for National Statistics. These professionals will be able to give you an insight into the market and buyer demographics in your area.
3. **Up-and-coming developments or community changes:** Get up to speed on any changes that are in motion in your area. Are there plans for new schools, shops or housing developments that are likely to change the demographic of the community?

The five main buyer profiles

There are five main buyer profiles: first-time buyer, upsizing family, downsizer, retiree and investor/professional. Below we'll look at each in turn, considering the key things that they are likely to want to have (or avoid) in their ideal property:

First-time buyer

- Potential for them to grow
- Social space
- Instagrammable style
- Space and light
- Safe investment
- Not too much maintenance
- Not tired or dark

Upsizing family

- Safe environment
- Space they can use
- Functional flow
- Connection to outdoor space
- Multifunctional rooms
- Storage availability
- Aspirational style
- Safe investment
- Not dark and closed

Downsizer

- Space for possessions and furniture
- Outdoor space
- Guest space
- Character
- Somewhere they can be proud of
- Not cramped
- Not suffocating (eg, trees in front of windows)

Retiree

- Space for possessions and furniture
- Outdoor space
- Guest space
- Character
- Light
- Not old-fashioned

Investor or professional

- Functional space
- Immediate use

- Opportunity to work/live/play
- Not too much work or maintenance
- Not crowded

CASE STUDY: UPSIZING FAMILY

The McCarthy family have a three-year-old son and are hoping to move from their current two-bedroom maisonette to give them more space and expand their family in the future. They love their current home, which feels comfortable and welcoming, but they dream of having a larger three-bedroom property to give them the space that they desire.

When viewing three-bedroom properties, their first judgement comes as they approach the home. Is it a safe environment for their son? They assess the structures: fences and gates, the road, the way that the property approaches the street and the space immediately outside the front door.

On entering the property, the McCarthy family will immediately want to see space in the hallway, and imagine entering with one or two children, a dog, a pushchair and all the bags from the school run. A cramped and dark hallway could be an immediate turn-off. You only have seven seconds to create a first impression, so if you do anything at all, get this entrance right. Seeing a spacious and clear hallway will not only give your buyer the immediate sense of space, but you will powerfully ease them into the viewing and welcome them to the home.

As the McCarthys stand in the hallway, they nervously review what they can see. Closed doors from the hallway keeps their attention in that space only. This can feel restricting, enhance tension and draw attention to every tiny detail, such as those little wall scuffs or a spider's web in the high corner. By throwing open the doors, you will allow them to experience the full space available on that floor. While a tiny action, this can be a game changer for a family who have come from a smaller home. By giving them a small glimpse into the other rooms, you will ignite a spark of excitement, drawing them in to explore the other spaces.

Moving through the home, the McCarthys snap out of that immediate excited burst, and focus on the practical elements of the home.

Does it have sufficient storage space for toys, household items, bikes and prams?

- Are the rooms in keeping with the day-to-day life of a growing family?
- Are the bedrooms big enough for their furniture, clothes and toys?
- Are the bathrooms in good condition or will they need to be replaced?
- Will the property need any work – is it too much of a project?

This is where you need to be aware of what they need, highlight anything that is a winning point and resolve any potential barriers. By doing so, you will keep their positive engagement throughout their viewing, giving them the ability to see their future and daydream a little about life to come. This is where your effective staging, organising, decluttering and refreshing decor is crucial. (We will cover this in greater detail later in the chapter.)

You can download more buyer profiles with key action points and your own home-staging action plan template from the online Happy Home Sale resource library at natalieevansuk.com

Enhancing the flow of your property

Whether buyers are scrolling through properties online or viewing in person, keeping the experience easy for your buyer is essential. The best way to capture their attention and maintain their focus is by perfecting the flow and purpose of each space in your home.

Imagine you're taking a riverboat ride. On a steady stream, you can move calmly along the river feeling positive and calm, observing everything around you from an optimistic place. You enter a kind of tranced state, where everything feels right. But if halfway down the river, something sticks out on the bank, or you hit a bump in the water, you will instantly snap out of your happy place. The disruption quickly becomes the defining part of your boat ride, with the calm and positive sensation lost.

It is just the same with a property viewing. It is amazing how a distraction can completely destroy a buyer's connection to a property. Whether it is one photo mid-scroll or one item on a viewing, the break from the flow can be a deal breaker. This could be something as small as a wilting plant, a vibrant wall colour, an unusual use for a room or even an empty space. Assessing the flow of your home and ensuring that each room has the correct purpose will help you get better results from viewings.

Here are some ways you can enhance the flow of your home:

- Opt for **a complementary colour scheme** throughout your home. If you have a neutral home but one bolder colour room, consider redecorating the stand-out room to bring it in line with the rest of the home. This will reduce the shock factor when the buyer enters the room and keep them in flow.
- If decorating is not an option, add a **hint of the bold colour** into the room directly before that one to blend the schemes. For example, if you have a neutral hallway but a wild pink bedroom, add some pink flowers in the hallway. This will gently ease your buyer into the bold colour and stop it being such a striking distraction.
- **Fix the little things** – dripping taps, snags in the carpet, creaking doors, etc. The tiniest snag can be a big deal. Think about what the dripping tap really tells the buyer: if that is faulty, what else has been

left uncared for? Your buyer can get swept away in unnecessary thoughts triggered by a small detail. By attending to the small things, you are reassuring your buyer that they are making a safe choice in their purchase and squashing any unnecessary worries.

- **Furnish any empty rooms** – empty rooms are incredibly hard to visualise. It is a common misconception that empty rooms look bigger. They look smaller, and this is a big distraction when it comes to viewings. Buyers spend more time trying to work out whether their furniture would fit than taking in the home's positive features. Use a home-staging professional to lease furniture to market your property or borrow furniture from a friend. This will show available space and keep your buyer engaged and excited in their viewing. If you don't know where to start with finding a home-staging expert, check the Home Staging Association directory: https://homestaging.org.uk
- Look at the original floor plan of your home and consider exactly **what your dream buyer needs**. Are all your rooms set out as originally intended? You may use

your dining room as an office, but your buyer needs to see the property as they would use it for maximum impact and flow. Dress it as a dining room. Keep in mind that the way that you use your home and the way that you need to stage it to sell are two different things.

CASE STUDY: STAGING THE KEY AREAS

The Nygh family's four-bedroom family home had been on the market for over a year, and despite being extremely spacious and in a great area, buyers were just not connecting with it. The Nygh family knew that something was blocking their sale and couldn't quite pinpoint the reason that they were struggling to get the interest they had expected.

Why? When living in the home, the Nyghs spent 99% of their time in a large kitchen–diner at the rear of the house. It was an incredible space and a regular hub for family and friends to enjoy dinners, parties and play dates. Their lifestyle was focused around socialising and dining with family and friends, and their design of the extension and use of the house represented that. They never used the front reception room, because they never lived in that way.

Over time, the room that would traditionally be the living room had become full of things – toys, storage units, a desk, a piano and fitness equipment.

When buyers looked at the home online, or attended viewings, they only ever saw a one-reception-room property. They saw a house with a large office and one open-plan room. Despite the front reception room being a generous size, the overcrowding and busy use of the room made it appear dark, small and confusing. Buyers can struggle to see the true availability of space when they are distracted by current use.

The turning point came when the Nygh family brought their dream buyer to their attention and restored the front reception room to its original purpose. Together, we created a plan to organise and stage their front room as the cosy, family living room that their buyer craved.

By presenting a harmonious flow from room to room and showing their dream buyer the home in a way that connected with their needs, they completely transformed their sale. Just five days after they added new images online, their offer came in. Their hard work fully paid off, and it is safe to say that they experienced the power of home staging.

Home staging on a budget

Often, when thinking about the idea of dressing or staging your home in preparation for it going on the market, people imagine the glamour of Netflix's *Selling Sunset* or other television shows depicting million-pound home transformations, but this is not always the case. Don't get me wrong, there are some incredible interior designers and home stagers out there who work on grand mansions and panoramic penthouses, but home staging is definitely not a service restricted to the rich and famous. Every homeowner needs to apply the foundations of home staging to kickstart their home sale, and you can do this without having to spend a small fortune.

In fact, it is incredible the number of items that you may already have in your home that can be repurposed to achieve what you need to without spending a single penny. We can become blind to the things that we have in our home. We get used to their location in certain rooms, on certain walls or their specific place on a certain window ledge. You know it's true. I have things in my own home that I don't even notice on a day-to-day basis, but, if you move them, I will see!

A neat idea is to start with a completely clean slate and re-dress your property from the mindset of your buyer. I call this 'express staging'. I advise homeowners to go around the house and take all ornaments, books, cushions, wall art, mirrors, artificial flowers and plants out of the rooms and put them away for a period of time. Once they are confident about who their dream buyer is and understand their key needs and wants when looking for a home, they can bring the items back out.

You will be blown away by the amount of inventory you have managed to collect without spending any money at all. By starting with this clean slate, you can use these items in a way that will truly connect with your dream buyer. Nothing has a set place. If, on reflection, something is better suited in another room then go ahead and use it in the new space.

There are three simple steps to express staging:

- Clear away
- Reassess
- Re-dress

This can often be a difficult task. If you find that you are just putting things back in the same space as before, do not worry. Ask for help.

Just last week, I was talking to a lady while in the queue for a coffee. (I talk to everyone I meet – I'm just 'that' person!) She had two children, one in university and another already settled in their own home. She knew that she would soon be looking to sell up and find a smaller home for her new life stage as an empty nester. While her target buyer was likely to be an older family, she laughed about the fact that they would be ten to fifteen years her junior and the difference a decade made. I couldn't believe how savvy she was. She already had plans to borrow pieces from a younger colleague who was in the same stage of life as her dream buyer.

This is an amazing idea. I have always found that people are happy to help, especially when they know what a difference it can make. Asking family and friends to lend furniture or accessories to help present your home for the right audience is a great move, especially when they are your dream target demographic.

CASE STUDY: STAGING FOR THE TARGET BUYER

A recent client of mine gave me a call out of the blue. I was pleased to see his name pop up on my phone, as we had staged his mother's home to sell earlier in the year with raging success, and it is always such a pleasure to catch up. He was full of great news. After separating before lockdown, he and his wife had decided to get back together and start a fresh life together in a new home with their family. It would be a fresh chapter for them both.

This meant him selling the previous family home that he had been living in post-split. Having experienced the success of staging his mother's home, he knew immediately that by investing time into fully preparing his home to go on the market, he would have maximum success and a happier selling experience.

While his home was in a prime family-friendly location, he knew that his more recent bachelor lifestyle was evident throughout the property, preventing a family from seeing how they may use the space in their future life. He was completely right. His home was a great size and in perfect condition, but it lacked the warmth and comfort that would ultimately make his dream buyer fall in love.

Following the three express staging steps above, and adding a few additional pieces of fragrance and greenery, the narrative of his home was transformed from bachelor pad to welcoming family home in under one day. It was a full-blown express staging event, with each family member taking ownership of a room and setting a timer to clear everything out. Creating a fun-filled game out of the task at hand brought excitement and competition in the house. The atmosphere was electric as they found treasures from past holidays, photos from special occasions and laughed as they shared stories along the way.

Once the rooms were cleared of photos, posters, plants, aftershave bottles and games consoles, they began thinking about the future of the home and reminiscing about when they had first moved in as a family, using the pieces that they had cleared away to re-dress each of the rooms. Better still, they packed up pieces that they weren't using to stage ready for their move and removed pieces they no longer wanted at the same time. Productive in every way.

Getting family and friends involved when you need help is key. Preparing your home can be a big job at times, and even when it doesn't involve heavy work, it can be overwhelming. Our homes are full of memories, stories and treasures, which can make the process difficult on your own. So why not join forces with a friend or member of the family to make it happen.

The trick to making this a happy experience is to remember your vision and align with others around you. You all have a role to play in achieving your next chapters, and coming together as one will bring you closer to your desires.

After a busy day clearing and staging, my client and his family reflected on their hard work and enjoyed a celebratory takeaway in the home that soon would become someone else's. For under £250, the home was ready for a powerful launch and the listing was up within just forty-eight hours.

Here is the power punch. Within twenty-four hours of launch, he had an offer for £12,000 over the asking price. The money that he invested into preparing his home meant that he effortlessly made £11,750. That is an additional dividend towards creating the abundant future that he dreamed of for his family.

The express staging steps are valuable to all, and by getting family and friends involved, you can create a beautiful event from something both physically and emotionally difficult. Whether your move to a new home is surrounded with excitement, or you're navigating your way through the loss of a loved one, stepping into the job at hand and working together will bring light to every circumstance.

I have worked alongside many homeowners who do not have family or friends around them for additional support when preparing their home, which is where bringing in a trusted professional can be extremely valuable. A key member of your dream team, a stager or organiser who can ride this journey with you towards your home sale will provide additional expertise and hands-on support when you need it. The more guidance you can get to steer your sale in the right direction, the less pressure you will feel throughout your selling journey.

Quick tips to prepare your home

To get you started with your own home staging and preparation, here are some simple tried-and-tested tips that I have put into action over the years to help clients boost the appeal of their home. While there are no one-size-fits-all tricks, they apply to most property styles and target buyer groups, so take note and see how you can use them in your preparation.

1. Never forget the hallway

- Create as much space as possible in the hallway and enhance the feel of light and space.
- Remove shoes, coats, bags, etc. Leave very little in the room.
- Where the decor is dark, consider repainting it with a light-reflecting colour.
- Leave the internal doors leading off the hallway open to give the buyer a teaser of what is coming up and draw them in both physically and emotionally.

2. Mirrors are your friend

- Use a mirror in your hallway to allow your buyer to literally visualise themselves coming into and leaving their new home.

- Think about the reflection. Don't place a mirror opposite a busy space, as it will reflect the chaos.

3. Clear the bathroom

- People judge on products and brand – remove all toiletries, including bottles of shampoo, perfume and other personal items from your bathroom.
- Clean the bathroom with lightly scented non-bleach products to provide a refreshing aroma that is not overwhelming.

4. Remove personal items

- Remove all your family photos, certificates and paperwork. Alongside protecting your personal information, the more you remove, the greater the opportunity you give your future buyer to see themselves in your home. Every second that they spend looking at your photos is a second of them not seeing the qualities of your home and how it can work for them.

5. Cupboards count

- Make sure that your kitchen cupboards, bathroom cabinets and built-in wardrobes are tidy.
- Many people think that cupboards are safe spaces to shove everything in, but viewers will look. If they see overcrowding and mess, this tells your prospective buyer that there is not enough storage.

6. Make the bed

- An unmade bed will give the impression that you do not care, that you aren't serious about selling. This is a big red flag and a turn-off for buyers.
- Head to my website, natalieevansuk.com to download a bed recipe to help you create that dream-worthy bedroom.

7. Leave a token

- If your home is in an aspirational location or has a link to a particular historical setting (eg, castle), geographical setting (eg, coast) or pastime (eg, yachting), then display a small token as a nod to this point.

- This could be as simple as leaving a copy of your local paper on the coffee table or relevant books in the office. Often a setting is a key selling point for a property, so use this to your advantage.

Home-selling Myth 3: My house is perfect without staging

I love my home. But that's because I decorated it to my taste, accessorised it in my style and used the spaces to suit my day-to-day life. If asked, I would say that it is perfect… for me.

It is essential to remember that you are not selling the house to yourself. You are selling it to another person, someone who is likely to be at a different stage of life, who has different needs, tastes and desires. While your home may be perfect for you today, the desired layout, colouring and use of space may not be right for your dream buyer. Every home needs to be assessed and tweaked to enhance its appeal, and by naively sitting in a 'my house is perfect' mentality, you'll be setting yourself up for a far more frustrating and prolonged selling experience than if you accepted your need to make some changes.

Summary

Your home is not about you anymore. Step out of your 'you' thinking and step into the mindset of the person who will make your dream offer.

Throughout this chapter, we have looked at why it is so important to make your home stand out to the right person. Stopping them in their tracks as they scroll online portals creates the best opportunity for them to fall head over heels at first sight of your property. By taking steps to prepare and stage your home, you can create a fun, enlightened and supportive experience to reflect on your memories and move on from any past stories that are no longer serving you as you go forward into your next chapter. Whether you make gentle edits or work with a trusted home stager to fully furnish a space, your investment will be significantly rewarding – not to mention less costly than reducing your asking price or taking a disappointingly low offer.

FOUR

Surviving Your Launch

Whenever I think of a property launching on the market, I think of the guys at NASA counting down 'Five, four, three, two, one… We have lift-off!', as if a team of engineers are ready to press a giant red button and catapult your home onto the market. While in reality the action of launching isn't quite so dramatic, it is a big day and certainly deserves acknowledgement as a significant milestone.

Your launch day should be agreed and set with your agent in advance, so there are no surprises. You want to know exactly when it will happen to be prepared physically and emotionally. This is the moment that you have been building up to for a while, so finding it emotional is normal. Don't suppress the feelings. Lean into them, breathe deeply, focus on your vision from chapter one, and remind yourself why you are selling. Your dream home, your new chapter, your goal is within touching distance and this launch propels you towards it.

This chapter is your launch survival guide. I'll talk you through this key milestone and prepare you for the next stages as you move towards the offer that you have been dreaming of. Together, we will steer your experience in the direction that you need to not only achieve a successful sale but guarantee a positive and stress-free experience.

If this is your first sale, or your first for a number of years, this process will be new for you. It can feel daunting, exciting and a whole mixed bag of emotions, but you are not alone. I guarantee that you will welcome your launch, breeze through your viewings and establish effective communication with your dream team, all of which will create a launch that works for you and gets you to faster sale success.

Let's recap on how far you've come. You have intentionally entered into your home-selling journey in a happy and mindful way, putting you on the path to securing the vision you've been dreaming of. This is no small feat, so celebrate that you are right here, ready to launch your home. Perhaps you felt that knee-jerk reaction kick in, screaming at you to ignore all the advice and throw your house on the market. You may have had a friend or even a local estate agent pressuring you to 'just go for it'. Perhaps you were tempted to jump a chapter or two because you cannot possibly wait one second longer. But remember everything that we have talked through. The pressure from others around us can be the number-one obstacle to your positive experience. The impulse to rush onto the market may be coming from an underlying issue which is waiting to prevent you from getting where you want. Stand tight and have confidence that you can create the sale that you so rightly deserve by being patient, prepared and ready. No pressure, no rush, just at the right time. Your offer is in touching distance.

I always imagine that the feeling of being fully prepared for anything in life is similar to that of an Olympic gold medal winner on the starting line. When you watch the Olympics, the focus, confidence and strength that you see in their eyes is powerful. They aren't on that line 'hoping' to get gold, 'trying' to achieve their goal, they are on the line already knowing that their dedication to training and passion for their sport has guaranteed that they will finish and walk away with a gold medal. They have no doubt. They know that they have done everything in their power for their best performance.

The same applies on your property launch day. Like the sound of a klaxon on the starting line, the call from your agent should bring you inner belief. You know that you are heading towards that finishing line, because you are serious about achieving it. You have your dream team by your side and your home is ready to capture the attention and heart of your ideal buyer. This is all you need, and this is exactly what you have. Your dedication to achieving your happiest home-selling journey is about to pay off, in a big way. Happy launch day!

Trust your estate agent

Homeowners often feel an eerie pause the moment they launch. The anticipation and build-up of the big day is followed by a second of silence. For the first time in this process, you have nothing to do but have confidence in your estate agent, to trust that they are taking the right actions to market your property and get it noticed by the right people.

Giving over this control can make sellers feel powerless, but this is why you did the hard work ahead of launch to bring your perfect estate agent into your dream team. Knowing that you have the best people for you by your side, sharing your vision to sell, puts you in an even more powerful position, and soothes any feelings of concern or doubt. Most of the time when you speak to someone who has experienced a tough sale, their number-one complaint relates to who they appointed on their team. They didn't take the time to get it right.

Having trust in your agent will be extremely valuable to you from the moment you launch and will shape your entire selling experience. A mutual understanding of how they work and how you need them to work will create perfect alignment for your home-selling process.

CASE STUDY: APPOINTING THE RIGHT AGENT

Mr and Mrs Bridge approached me in 2021 needing help with the sale of their holiday home. Their pastel pink cottage was a true sight of English country garden elegance with an extremely characterful interior – exposed brickwork, timber beams and an open fireplace to fulfil the picture-perfect cosy cottage dream.

But prospective buyers were unable to see it. The beautiful detailing was overpowered by their collection of mismatched furniture, which saw the cottage sitting unsold on the market for eighteen months. Even just writing that, I can feel myself in complete shock that something with such incredible potential could be so overlooked on the market for such a long period of time.

What blows my mind is that the acting agent had not thought to do anything to address this other than reduce the price. Mr and Mrs Bridge were completely backed into a corner, having been told to reduce the price time and again, to the point that they could not afford to reduce any further. Over time, communication from their agent dwindled, and any calls to request updates were not returned. But being the closest agent to the cottage and highly recommended by neighbours, the Bridges felt that they had to remain with them.

After delving into Mr and Mrs Bridge's situation, it was clear to see what had happened: they had followed the decisions of others around them and enlisted an agent that did not fit their needs. While they were a reputable national chain with a sales team, the agent specialised in lettings. They simply did not have the right database or marketing available to get the cottage in front of the second homeowner or investor buyers who this cottage was best suited to. In addition, the limited experience of the sales team meant that they had no remedy to aid their slow sale other than price reduction. Instead, they placed the cottage on one online property platform, and left it sitting there month after month hoping that the right buyer would find it.

It was time for a relaunch. The Bridges needed to boost the cottage's appeal and bring it back onto the property market with a new agent who had the tools available to give it the exposure it deserved.

The cottage was fully staged, additional furniture added and fresh accessories placed to make sure it stood out and presented a vision of idyllic cottage life. The combination of refreshed marketing and new agent attracted enough interest to book out a relaunch weekend. Less than two weeks after staging and relaunching, the property had received multiple offers, giving Mr and Mrs Bridge the freedom to select the best offer for them.

The biggest warning sign for Mr and Mrs Bridge was reduced agent communication. Being ignored, receiving limited updates or having zero communication with your agent is a sure sign that they could be struggling to deliver the services that they initially promised or expected.

Appointing an agent

When setting out on your journey with your agent, you need to be crystal clear about your mutual boundaries and expectations. Ask them the following questions:

- What communication should you expect from them?

- How often will they update you?
- What happens if they do not deliver?

There is nothing more concerning for you as a homeowner than feeling left in the dark. Likewise, there is nothing more frustrating for an agent than being hounded ten times a day. Identify exactly what you can expect and when, so that you can ease your mind and give your agent the space to do their job.

Sometimes, as with the above case study, the communication levels are not addressed and lead to poor performance. But how can you overcome this?

My number-one recommendation to anyone who finds themselves in this position is to have an honest conversation with their agent. Be confident and professional, and arrange a face-to-face meeting with them. Everyone in your dream team should be working with you to achieve your vision, not working against you. If at any point you feel ill-informed, concerned or distrustful, a personal meeting is the best way forward.

Reviewing your agent

Ask your agent for an honest review of the way that they are working. Ask why you haven't been receiving information and whether they have any concerns about their ability to achieve the sale you need.

Understanding and compassion are powerful tools in these situations. All agents have different markets, audiences and strengths. By showing awareness of this, you will be able to demonstrate your understanding of their role, and that you are not disrespecting their efforts but purely seeking the confidence that they are truly the best agent to sell your home.

Still not convinced? Then try this power phrase: 'If you aren't able to or don't currently have the means to effectively market my property to get an offer, that is OK. But I wish to be released from my contract to give me the opportunity to sell and to allow you to focus on other properties.'

Always review your contract and identify the routes available to you to exit. Where appropriate, seek legal advice. Do not get angry, confrontational or pushy, but do stand confident in the knowledge that you need to have the right team around you to deliver the result you expect.

A bad experience does not mean that they are a bad agent. They are just not the best fit for your sale. Most of the time, a gentle refocus and honest conversation can get everyone realigned and on track. In fact, some of the best ideas and proposals come from these conversations. You and your agent are in this together, so honest, collaborative communication often ends in a great result – even if the outcome is to move on to another, more suitable agent. Knowing that you are back on track with the right agent partner will bring so much ease for the rest of your home-selling journey.

Keep things moving

I hear so many stories of property launches, some of overwhelm and some of radio silence. There is such a mixture of experiences, but the greatest position to be in is one where you are prepared for quick change. At times you may be met with a lull in interest and your positivity and confidence will be the driver to keep things moving forward.

When things seem slower, be proactive. Use these times to think about yourself, take time to review your vision and practise self-care. Don't get lost in questions of doubt – these will never serve you and will certainly escalate when you are unable to drive activity. I often hear comments that begin with 'I don't understand why' or 'If I were the agent', followed by negative assumptions. These hypothetical messages of negativity will not help you and often put sellers in a fearful, frustrated position. Experiencing fleeting feelings of uncertainty is perfectly normal. After all, you have been heavily involved in everything so far, and being away from the action can be unnerving. But have faith in the hard work and preparation that you have committed so far. This will pull you away from becoming lost in any unnecessary anxiety.

Trust me, you will be pleased for having taken the pause when the busy period hits – because it will. It may be a few days or weeks, but with the right agent, right price and right presentation, your home is sure to command attention.

When viewings start getting booked in, it can feel overwhelming, especially if you get trapped in a cycle of preparing your home at short notice, day in and day out. Prospective buyers can come back two, three or even four times before settling on a final decision and once they have made an offer, they will want to come back to measure up, bring family or just settle their mind that they have made the right decision. One viewer could visit up to five times. Imagine if you have ten interested parties. That's ten appointments for the initial round of viewings alone and up to fifty overall.

The key to staying on top of this is to think about how to manage the busy times, and how to protect your time. If each viewing means dropping the kids to childcare, finding someone to dog-sit and cleaning for an hour as well as managing a full-time job, then you are quickly going to find viewings overwhelming. Later in the chapter, I will share some top tips to help you be ready with little effort, but for now, let's think about how you can protect yourself and your time.

Effective time management

An agent once told me that the answer to achieving a fast sale was to get as many people in the door as possible. They then went on to describe the sheer number of people that they book in for short slots. This theory was similar to that of the old phrase 'throw mud at a wall and see if it sticks', arranging high-volume viewings with hope of a quick offer. I can tell you now, this is absolutely *not* the best way to sell your home. The most successful viewing strategy is to invite only serious, targeted and relevant buyers to your property.

There is nothing worse than booking in dozens of viewings, only to find that the prospective buyers 'didn't want a flat' or were 'really wanting a house out of town'. Make sure that your agent is vetting potential buyers, and be strict that if they are not in a position to buy, if they don't have confirmed finances and if they aren't a true match for your home, then they cannot view.

Your time is precious, and you want to be sure that the hours you are investing in preparing your home, family life, personal life and work schedule to accommodate a viewing is worth your while. It may take the agent longer, but you will be in a far stronger position to sell by having three serious viewings rather than twenty casual viewers. Your time is worth more than just 'throwing mud', so don't ever get caught in that trap.

When I was selling our family home, despite working with a great agent, we still had 'curious' viewers. You know the ones – they have no interest in actually buying your house but would just like a look. By knowing that your agent is on your side and is only inviting genuinely validated buyers, you will have the capacity, the time and mental focus to be ready for their viewings. This is the stronger strategy. Do not waste your effort on casual, curious viewers who are never going to buy your home.

One day, after our home launch, I got a call from our estate agent. A prospective buyer had called in to say that they had seen our house while they were on their lunch break and were hoping to go across immediately to view. A sudden rush of excitement and adrenaline hit me, followed by dread. I was at work and was certainly not ready for a viewing at that short notice.

As you know, I had taken time to stage and prepare our house for the marketing photography and generally left it clean and tidy on a day-to-day basis. But I wanted to make sure that our house was perfect for whoever came, and I was pretty sure that in the rush to work that morning, I would have left the children's pyjamas on the bed unfolded, and smudges in the shower from washing my hair. This was not how I wanted my house to be seen.

You have to love keen buyers. But sometimes the fierce need to drop everything and allow them an immediate viewing can be overwhelming. Remember, it is OK to set boundaries and say no, even in a buyer's market. As I write this book, the property market is hot, but there are not a lot of properties on the market, so this is what we would refer to as a seller's market. In a hot seller's market, you are in a great position to set your boundaries and conduct viewings on your terms. By keeping everything calm and taking time to prepare correctly, you can be sure to give the best impression and experience for your prospective buyer. After all, we all know that first impressions count, *not* fast impressions.

Arranging viewings

Let's think about this in a little more detail. Can you guarantee that all viewings are booked on your terms and that all prospective buyers get to see your home in the best light, first time?

Think about what you need to give you the time, space and clarity to prepare your home. Here are some things to consider:

- Would your viewings be better conducted at a certain time of the day, perhaps in school hours?
- Would a specific day of the week suit you better?
- How much notice do you need to allow you to arrange a cleaner or dog-sitter?
- Do you have any personal commitments that make some days or times unsuitable?

While we want your future buyer to be happy, I am here to remind you that *you* need to have a happy journey through this sale. You have the right to set these boundaries, and getting exactly what you need down on paper will help you set them. Be sure to communicate these needs clearly with your agent. You may want to discuss it with them in person and follow up on email. It doesn't matter how you do it. Just be confident to set your boundaries.

You may be greeted with suggestions from your agent, or possibly get a call at a later stage that goes against the boundaries you set. Stand firm. There is a reason why you set your terms and you are within your rights to do so.

View your house as your buyer would

I always recommend that where possible, you visit your home immediately before a viewing to stroll through each room. This makes sure that you are truly giving your dream buyer the space and opportunity to see their future in your home. I like to take a slow walk, starting at the front door and stopping in each space to think about what a viewer will see, hear, smell and experience as they come in for the first time.

Look around and see what your eye is drawn to. If it is something that needs tidying, then take a few moments to correct it and then return to the point you were at. Once you have been around the house, push open the doors leading off the hallway and let a little fresh air into the space.

Make sure you have left the property twenty minutes before the viewing. Your viewer may come a little early, and it is always more comfortable to leave the introductions and tour to your agent.

Sometimes it is not possible to check your home before a viewing. To help you out here is my daily 'just in case' checklist, to make sure you have done the viewing essentials before you leave the house. This way, you will be prepared for a viewing at any point in the day while you are out.

EXERCISE: DAILY 'JUST IN CASE' CHECKLIST

- Clear the hallway. Make sure all shoes are away and that the hallway is clear and tidy.
- Put the washing up away. Wash and put away all the plates and pots from breakfast and the night before, leaving the sink, sides and draining board clear.
- Remove distracting rubbish and laundry. Take out the bins, and make sure clothes are

folded and put away. One of my pet hates on Rightmove is seeing a clothes airer.

- Flush the toilets. Flush them all.
- Make the beds. Take time to make all the beds before leaving in the morning.

These small tasks will put you in a much better position for a viewing, especially if something does arise last minute. You are not alone in this sale, so ask for help where you can. Share the jobs among your family or bring in the support of a home-staging professional. And, yes, flush the toilet. 'The house with the dirty toilet' is not the impression you want to leave.

Be open to feedback

Like everything in life, some things suit some people and some things don't, and that's OK. But we are not great at receiving and accepting feedback as a positive thing. People avoid feedback as a way of protecting themselves. Today is the day that we change this misconception and open ourselves to hearing it. Because by receiving feedback in all areas of our lives, we grow stronger.

When selling your home, listening to viewing feedback is key – both positive and negative.

Getting clear, structured and relevant feedback about your home from the perspective of your potential buyer is one of the most valuable tools available to you. Ask for it, embrace it and welcome it.

Clear and constructive feedback gives you the building blocks to guarantee your success in the next viewing for absolutely free! It shows you how your property is being perceived and the steps you can take to guarantee that the right impression is created for your next viewer.

So, never shy away from it. In fact, I recommend putting a system in place with your estate agent early in your selling journey to make sure that you get feedback in a timely manner. Take time to listen to the feedback and decipher what it is *really* telling you. Once you have identified any sticking points for potential buyers, you can minimise any barriers in time for your next viewing. You will be in an informed position to get the offer you deserve.

I talk about this so often. Whenever I meet someone who is going through a slow or struggling sale, I'll ask them, 'What is blocking you from selling? What has the feedback been?' and most of the time I am met with this response: 'I don't know.'

I'll then ask, 'Have you asked your agent for the information?', and they always reply that they have, but the agent wasn't able to tell them anything. I can guarantee that in all cases, they have not had the conversation with the agent for feedback or have not set out the expectation that they want honest, constructive feedback. If they had, they would not have become so stuck.

Home sales are going on all around us, all the time, and it never ceases to amaze me how many people I accidentally speak to who turn out to be on the market or about to launch. When I started writing this book, I met a wonderful book coach, Monique. Monique worked with me to get my ideas, stories and tips into a coherent flow. She was so engaged throughout our conversations because she was in the process of selling her mother's home. As we spoke about viewings and feedback, I could tell that she had a story to tell, and I am so pleased to be able to share it with you here because it really highlights the importance of listening to your feedback.

CASE STUDY: RESPONDING TO FEEDBACK FROM BUYERS

After Monique's mother had completed a handful of viewings on her home, a few prospective buyers had commented that they were put off by how it looked from the kerb. The house was lovely with a large character front window. But immediately in front of it was an oversized camellia bush.

While her agent had been very clear in delivering their feedback, Monique's mother refused to listen. She would tidy the front lawn and trim the shrubs, but she refused to touch the camellia. Her family knew that she loved the camellia bush, having planted it herself many years before, but they could see that it was blocking her sale.

Sometimes feedback will come to you in a crystal-clear way, showing you exactly what you need to do to capture the interest of your buyer. Sometimes it will be something that you don't want to hear, but as with the camellia bush, it can prevent you from selling. It is so important to step out of your emotional mindset, listen to the feedback and take action as needed.

Once the bush was down, the response to Monique's mother's property was staggering. Viewings were being booked in faster than before, which achieved competing offers. Listening to the feedback saved her sale and allowed Monique's mother to move on to her new home where, in no time, she planted a new camellia.

Delivering the best viewing experience

Here are some tips to give your property the best chance to shine:

- I am a huge pet lover, but when it comes to a property viewing, your handsome hound is a no-no. Make sure that your home is free of pet toys, blankets, food bowls, fur, litter and, most importantly, poop! Make sure that your home is pet free. Pets can be a huge turn-off for house hunters, who may either dislike pets or get distracted by their presence.
- Tidy the toys. Children's plastic toys come in so many colours and sizes that even the best efforts to organise them can look a

mess. Invest in a tub and put *all* toys away in the wardrobe, garage or attic, out of sight. This will reduce any feeling of chaos and enhance the appearance of space in the room.

- Put all your bathroom products away and fully out of sight. No shampoo, soap or toothpaste allowed on viewings, please!
- Do not be tempted to use heavily scented products to clean before a viewing. Opt for lighter, fresher fragrances to make sure that the property is clean but not clinical.
- Where possible, open your window ahead of a viewing to let fresh air into the space. It is amazing the impact that this has on the overall experience.
- Get every last detail right, including sound. If you know a viewing is at peak traffic time, close the windows beforehand. Make sure that the washing machine isn't beeping and that taps aren't dripping. These sensory triggers can interrupt the ambience and flow of a viewing.

Home-selling Myth 4: Spring is the only season to sell

Let me tell you this right now, there is no fixed date in the calendar that is more favourable for going on the market. For years, we have believed that placing a property on the market in spring leads to a boost in sales activity, but over the past few years, the trend has leant towards a winter sale. In fact, the busiest period for online property searches is between Christmas and New Year.[3]

But remember, all this data is taken from national and local averages, and while we can look at them to get an indication of trends, it is not the same for every property. As you know from preparing your home for marketing, every target buyer is different. This not only applies to their property expectations but in their buying patterns. A family may be busier over the school holidays, actively house-hunting in term time, while a couple may choose to seek a fresh start for the new

3 'Rightmove claims new records for activity over Christmas', EstateAgentTODAY (January 2022), www.estateagenttoday.co.uk/breaking-news/2022/1/rightmove-claims-new-records-for-buyerseller-activity-over-christmas, accessed 30 March 2022

year. There is no real pattern for success. There is only the success that you create.

The perfect time to get your house on the market is when *you* have completed all the actions necessary to make the best decisions, select the right dream team and prepare your home for your dream buyer. Whether that is in March, September or December makes no odds. You're in control of your launch.

Summary

In this chapter, we have looked at how to get your launch off to the right start and how to get your property – and yourself – ready for viewings in a stress-free way that is compatible with your work and life demands. We have talked about how to appoint an agent and how to set out what you expect from them, and them from you. We have considered how your buyers will see your property and have a list of actions we can take to show your property in its best light. We have also discussed the importance of feedback and opening yourself up to making any changes needed to transform your sale. You are now in the strongest position to get your property on the market and take that leap towards achieving the offer you have been dreaming of.

The next step is to celebrate your success. Are you ready?

FIVE
Celebrate Your Offer

It's time to celebrate. A buyer has made an offer on your home and everything that you have worked towards is paying off. We still have a few steps to take, but the news of your offer is something to be celebrated. Together we can make sure that the next phase of your home-selling journey continues to be filled with positivity and inspiration.

This chapter will talk you through the steps between receiving your offer and finally exchanging contracts. I'm going to be honest with you, some parts are going to be heavy. We will cover several eventualities that homeowners experience in this phase. I want you to be aware of all possible outcomes, not to fill you with fear but to fill you with knowledge. Most of the anxiety that comes from this stage in your selling journey stems from dealing with the unknown. People experience so many different situations that they have never needed to consider before that it is easy to feel ground down by it all. But I am here with you. I may not be able to solve every detail, but I can arm you with the tools to be able to manage them in a happier and less stressful way.

Processing your offer

Let's take you back to the moment you received your offer. The phone rang and your agent told you that an offer – heck, multiple offers – had been received. I know all too well the rush and exhilaration that this call would have brought you. And you deserved it! You worked monumentally hard to achieve this offer. From having the patience to assess your reasons for selling, to selecting your key agent, every aspect of your preparation paid off. But, tell me, how are you feeling now? Bewildered? Relieved? Terrified?

Every homeowner experiences different emotions when they receive an offer. It's understandable because everyone has a different reason for selling and experiences different situations along the way. An offer call that could be full of excitement and optimism for one person may be filled with fear and sadness for another. Whatever you are feeling when you receive the news, remember it's absolutely normal. Lean into whatever you are feeling. By connecting with your emotions, you will create space to process them and, if needed, heal. Take your time to feel any emotions that arise, and only once you are ready should you reflect on what this offer means to you and your next chapter.

Even the most positive and confident home sellers feel apprehensive when they receive an offer. Why? Let's go right back to where we started and remember the stories that we were told by family, friends and strangers about selling a home. Did you ever hear someone tell a wonderfully positive story about how smoothly their sale progressed to exchange? No, I didn't think so. People love to share stories of their drama – slow, painful solicitors, collapsing chains and so on. I'm not going to lie to you and pretend that every offer progresses swimmingly, but I will say that if everything went wrong every time, no one would ever sell their home!

There is always a chance of complication in anything we do, but you have a strong dream team, you have focus and you have me here 100% cheering you along. You've smashed it so far, and you can keep going.

Fear of a failed sale is real for so many people, and can completely cripple their selling experience. In fact, many cannot face celebrating the news for fear of everything going horribly wrong. Earlier this year, I had the pleasure of working with a wonderful couple, staging their apartment to go on the market after they had relocated. Their experience of selling up till then had been hit and miss, but staging gave the apartment a new boost of appeal, and in no time they had an offer on the table. They quickly accepted it and just wanted everything to progress as quickly as possible.

I am client-focused, and so is my team, so it is not uncommon for us to check in with each of our clients throughout the week. We love to talk through how their sale is progressing, or in the quieter weeks before exchange, have a casual catch-up. But it was noticeable that our apartment client was extremely quiet. She had gone from regularly calling and emailing to not being around at all.

I managed to speak to her one morning, and we spent over an hour talking about her offer. She said that she was trying to avoid everything about it, as she was so tremendously scared of jinxing it. She hoped to block it out and was suppressing every naturally arising emotion until she knew that the sale had completed. Each day she woke up with an underlying worry, which continued and stayed with her until everything was complete eleven weeks later.

Eleven weeks of upset, fear and anxiety. You cannot control any complications that arise in the later stages of your sale, but you can control how you experience it. Allow yourself to accept that things can go off track, but have confidence that they can quickly be realigned and put back on course. This will allow you to say goodbye to any fears and anxieties along the way. Every day, when walking down the street, we risk tripping up. But that doesn't mean that we are fearful every time we leave the house. We know and accept that sometimes we trip, but we'll get back up again.

I warned you that we would touch on some heavy points in this chapter, and it is vital that we can stand strong and accept that things occasionally go wrong. But by being OK with that, we will face no surprises.

Dealing with the unexpected

According to the UK Office for National Statistics, 40% of buyers pull out of the process after placing an offer. Let's digest that and accept that that can be a reality in this process. But this also means that 60% of buyers complete on their sale as planned. The odds are in your favour. Your dream team are ready to support you in preventing sale complications and giving you the confidence that should anything happen, you can and will get back on track.

CASE STUDY: WHEN A BUYER PULLS OUT

We worked with a gentleman, Tom, preparing his home to go on the market.

After launching, several offers came in very quickly, and within forty-eight hours, he had accepted one. Everything progressed seamlessly, with all the usual boxes ticked off: Proof of mortgage and ID presented, solicitors appointed, paperwork completed, mortgage valuation done, survey conducted. The buyer had even popped back several times to measure for furniture and curtains.

It was all looking great until the day before the contracts were exchanged. A shocking call to Tom revealed that after last-minute reconsideration, the buyer had changed their mind and had decided to withdraw from the purchase.

After back-and-forth conversations and negotiations to try and save the sale, the buyer didn't want to proceed. They'd had 'a change of heart'. It seemed unbelievable, especially after they had come so far in the process.

Tom was overwhelmed with feelings of anger and frustration. However, he knew that anger wouldn't solve anything. Working closely with his agent and solicitor, Tom was ready to jump back on the market. The agent reconnected with buyers who had previously offered and those on their database who fit the profile.

> Within just days, the property was back under offer and progressing with a new buyer. Having got to such a late stage first time round, his solicitor already had paperwork prepared, speeding up the process and progressing to exchange and onward completion within six weeks. While extremely frustrating, Tom's level-headed attitude meant that he was able to refocus and take the right steps to get everything back on track.

A focused and positive mindset is highly effective when navigating a potentially devastating situation. It is important to accept that these situations are possible and understand the steps to take should you hit a barrier. That way, if a problem arises, you will be ready both emotionally and strategically. Have confidence that even in the situation of a failed sale, you have achieved an offer already. You know the steps to take and you know that your home has appeal. Every step that we have worked through together so far has been designed to give you the resilience to face any hurdles and jump quickly back on the market to get the result you deserve.

If the sale fails because of something property-related, such as something flagged in the survey or in the leasehold agreement, take it as a gift, something you can learn and correct. Whether that means altering the price to cater for required work, or better communicating elements of a lease to prospective buyers, you know about this barrier now. Correct it and if you need to, relaunch and get another offer. You can do it!

At times, difficulties may arise from your side. From navigating mortgage complications to problems with your onward purchase, your dream team will be your lifeline when faced with a troublesome situation. They will have experienced every eventuality you could find yourself in, so fall back on their expertise and accept their support. It is in circumstances like this that you will be thankful for the time and energy that you put into finding the right people for your dream team.

Why do sales fall through?

In their 2017 paper *Research on Buying and Selling Homes,* The UK Department for Business, Energy and Industrial Strategy presented the various reasons that sales fall through and at what frequency.[4]

Reason	Frequency
Withdrew offer for personal reasons	17%
Withdrew following a survey that showed problems	16%
Another buyer made a better offer (gazumped)	13%
The seller withdrew without explanation	10%
Problem elsewhere in the chain	9%
Other seller related reasons	8%
The seller hadn't found a property or accommodation	6%
Didn't have sufficient funds/the lender would not agree the funds needed	5%
Leasehold related issues	4%
Other reasons	12%

Frustratingly, their findings showed that the highest percentage of failed sales (17%) comes down to one thing: the buyer's 'personal reasons'. We know from all the work that you

4 Department for Business, Energy and Industrial Strategy, 'Research on buying and selling homes' (October 2017), https://assets.publishing.service.gov.uk/government/uploads/system/uploads/attachment_data/file/653581/buying-selling_homes-research.pdf, accessed 30 March 2022

did in chapter one that people often enter into buying and selling homes without being truly ready. The knee-jerk reaction to buy or sell is real, and often has consequences later in the process.

It may feel as though things like this are out of your control, but this is not the case. Let's remind ourselves of the ways you have already taken some big steps to reduce the risk of the buyer's 'personal reasons' getting in the way of your sale:

- You have chosen an agent who is working with serious buyers only.
- You have selected a solicitor whom you trust to work effectively and efficiently.
- You have only invited validated and serious buyers to viewings.
- You have considered your reasons for buying your next home.
- You have determined your financial situation.
- You get to choose which offer you accept.
- You are in control.

Accepting your offer – or not

Many people believe that you should accept an offer as soon as you receive it, and that you should always accept an offer that is over your asking price. No. You should accept the best offer that has the greatest chance of successfully progressing to completion.

No matter what other people tell you, you do not have to accept an offer if it doesn't feel right, even if it is at your guide price. You can continue marketing your property for more offers until you are completely satisfied with the offer you receive.

Take this example. If you receive two offers, one offer at £5k less than the asking price and another at £5k over, your immediate thought may be to take the higher offer. But the buyers' circumstances could turn this on its head. If the first buyer is a cash buyer with no chain and the second buyer is purchasing with a mortgage and needs to sell their home, the first buyer comes with less potential risk. They don't have a mortgage application to navigate and are not dependent on another sale to proceed.

There are many things to consider before jumping to accept an offer, and by assessing the best offer to accept, you will put yourself in a stronger position for completing your sale. Your agent will have the relevant information, and while they are unable to tell you which offer to accept, they can advise on the potential outcomes for each buyer's situation.

Assessing your buyer

The following questions will help you decide whether to proceed with the buyer offering on your property:

- Does the buyer seem keen? Have they visited your home on several occasions? Did they come with family? Did they take photos? A more reliable, invested buyer will visit regularly and show signs of interest.
- Has the agent checked and validated your prospective buyer's finances? Are they taking out a mortgage? What is their deposit value? Have they completed a pre-mortgage application or had an agreement in principle from a lender? Has your agent seen the agreement in principle

letter? Does the amount cover the value of your home?

- Do your prospective buyers need to sell a property in order to buy yours? Do they already have an offer and a buyer lined up for their sale? How far along are they in that process? How many people are in their chain?
- Does the buyer have a history of withdrawing from a sale? Is there anything about their offer that doesn't sit quite right?

Getting the full picture on each offer will result in a much smoother road to completion, so take the time you need to decide the matter on your terms. The right offer for you may not be the conventional one. The most important thing to remember is that you are in control, no one can rush you. Stand your ground, take your time and be confident that you will make the right choice.

Waiting for completion

In the UK, regardless of whether or not we are in a seller's market, the average time from offer to exchange of contracts is nine weeks, with an additional two weeks between exchange of contracts and completion.[5]

Let's assume that you have eleven weeks to wait. This is a long time, and that's why things can feel slow. But there is a lot that goes on behind the scenes during this phase, so let's be realistic and not kid ourselves that the process will miraculously be turned around overnight. Instead, appreciate the work that is being completed for you during this time, getting you to where you want to be. Use this time to set the next steps of your sale process in motion, complete your move and close this chapter of your life.

I love reflecting on my experiences of buying and selling homes. My first experience was the purchase of a small flat and at that time, I didn't know a single thing about buying a property. I just offered and then, eleven weeks later, moved in. I didn't know anyone who had bought or sold so wasn't aware of the dreaded horror stories.

---

5 'Selling a house timeline', strike (nd), https://strike.co.uk/selling/selling-a-house-timeline, accessed 30 March 2022

My second experience was different. I was a little older and surrounded by homeowning friends. The period between offer and exchange felt long. It was anxiety-filled and frustrating. Every morning I craved an update. I felt angry to be out of the loop and found the entire experience pressured and uncertain. I hated every second. Why was I so worried? Because no one told me not to be, and I did not feel as though I had the support team around me that you do today.

The period between offer and completion may seem slow and quiet, but it should never feel upsetting or distressing. In fact, it can be a wonderful time for reflection. It gives you an opportunity to look back at how far you've come and refocus on where you are going.

EXERCISE: FIND A MINDSET ACTIVITY

Just as Tom Daley used his knitting to support his mindset in the 2021 Olympics, finding a calm yet focused activity for the eleven weeks between offer and completion will give you a beautifully positive outlet for staying grounded and happy. Here are some ideas of activities that may bring comfort while you're in the midst of your sale's progression:

- **Daily meditation.** Take time each morning to meditate, focusing on positivity in your journey, gratitude for moving towards your goal and visualising where you will be once your sale has completed.
- **Craft.** Knitting, sewing, painting and jewellery-making are all great activities that can keep your mind stimulated during a period of emotional pressure.
- **Sorting.** Get ahead of your move in a positive and creative way. Sort photos, create albums and organise clothes. Sorting and organising is a great way to naturally boost your mood and provide relief to any stress and anxiety.
- **Learning a new skill.** Whether languages, instruments, computer code or even mastering a Rubik's cube, learning a new skill can be a fun way to distract your mind.
- **Walking.** There is nothing better than fresh air for self-care. Getting your 10,000 steps a day is not only good for the waistline but amazing for your brain and for developing a positive outlook.
- **Exercise.** Set a fitness goal. A lot can be achieved in eleven weeks. In fact, the NHS provides a free online 'Couch to 5k' plan that you can complete in just nine weeks.[6]

---

6 NHS UK, 'Get running with Couch to 5k' (October 2020), www.nhs.uk/live-well/exercise/running-and-aerobic-exercises/get-running-with-couch-to-5k, accessed 30 March 2022

> That *would* be a positive and impressive achievement.

You're close now, and by trying one of these ideas, your happy ending will feel even closer.

Struggling to focus?

If you struggle to keep focus and find that negative thoughts of your sale constantly slip to the forefront of your mind, do not worry. I know it can be tough. The human mind is designed to protect you, and one way that it does this is by showing you thoughts, stories or ideas that make you feel fearful. It's as though your mind is telling you, 'Hey, friend. It's all going to go wrong – just accept it now and it won't hurt so badly when it happens.'

I have a solution for this that works in all areas of life when your loving but unhelpful mind is feeding you some fear. You are going to need to trust me on this one, OK? Whenever I experience any fearful thoughts that aren't serving me, I see them, I thank them and I release them. Yes, I go as far as thanking them out loud.

When your anxiety-inducing thoughts pop up, you could say something along the lines of, 'Thank you for showing me these fearful thoughts and for trying to protect me. I am happy and confident that I am closer to achieving my sale each day. I am supported, guided and know where I am going. My dream team is with me and I know that I have the power to create the life I desire.'

Once you have thanked the fear, push it away. You do not need it. Your main goal at this time is to stay focused on your vision as you get ever closer to achieving it.

Home-selling Myth 5: Get the highest offer you can – it's all about the money

Let's stamp this myth out right now. First, you do not have to do anything at all. Choosing the offer that is best for you is a personal decision, based on your assessment of the offers that you have received and knowing the full picture about your buyer. You should never feel pushed, forced or influenced to make a decision, especially if this advice is solely based on the value of the offer that you have received.

Remember, anyone can make an offer. Without understanding the full picture behind the offer, it is valueless. Someone could offer you £100k more than you were looking for. Imagine that. But the truth may be that they are not ready to buy and their inflated offer is as good as nothing.

The highest offer is not always the most valuable, financially speaking. Get the information you need to make the best decision for you. The offer you choose from an informed position is the one that will bring the happiest outcome.

Summary

Throughout this chapter, we have celebrated the offer – or offers – that you have on the table and looked at how to identify which will best serve you in achieving a smooth completion. The road to exchange can feel unnerving, but by having confidence in the buyer and in the dream team you have selected, you'll be unstoppable.

We know that at times, a sale can go off track. But while these derailments can feel devastating, the truth is that with these bumps in the road, there can come lessons for you that get you straight back on track. By focusing on where you are going, you can ride through this phase of your selling journey and arrive at exchange day in a calm and collected way.

Are you ready to get moving?

SIX

Let's Get Moving

The big day is nearly here! It's really happening. You have reason to be excited, but there is still work to do. The time has come to start getting the foundations in place for your move. With just a few weeks left until your sale is complete, now is the time to get busy.

We'll start by planning the actions to take to create your smoothest possible completion day. I am all about preparation, which is why I have dedicated a whole chapter to getting you moving. Pinpointing where to start can feel like a challenge, but this chapter will guide you through each step and give you the support you need to tackle them in a fun, inspiring and productive way. I want you to reach your exchange date knowing that 99% of the sorting, packing and preparing is done. That way, you can sit back happy and calm as your completion takes place.

Just as you may have been getting used to the quiet period after your offer, the pace shifts and it is action stations. Time to go go go! Many people feel comforted by the idea of getting busy at this stage. It brings relief to feel that something is happening and reassurance that they are close to getting to where they want to be.

The key is to be busy, but not overworked. Productive, but not overwhelmed. I often speak to clients who on first impression are excited to sort, pack and move, but when they realise the volume of work to be done, the pressure hits them. They quickly lose focus and sink into a state of overwhelm, leaving things closer and closer to completion. What is the result of that? Stress and panic. The positive selling journey now feels pressured, shifting them from a calm and happy state to feeling like they are drowning.

With focus, planning and action, this does not have to be a stressful time. In fact, by stripping back the weight of the work and planning each step, you will see this final hurdle as reflective and inspiring.

Your action stations checklist

I would love to tell you that there is a quick-fix solution to packing your house, or that I have a free downloadable magic wand that gets the job done for you. But the best tools for you at this stage are time, planning and teamwork.

Whether you are selling an apartment, your family home or the home of a loved one, putting time into sorting, packing and rehoming items where needed is extremely valuable. The earlier you can start getting these steps in motion, the sooner you will feel the reward. There are a few tricks to make this process fun along the way, which I will share with you throughout this chapter, but for now, grab a notepad and start by dating the top of the page, because we are going to get started right away.

Creating a full-blown action stations checklist is going to get everything you need to do down on paper, so nothing can be missed, forgotten or ignored (guilty!). Face the facts, and list the jobs. This will put you in a position of power and control, and I promise you, stress and fear will not *dare* raise their heads when you are in a strong mindset.

Let's look at how you can build this list. It's a simple technique, and one that works for so many things. After mastering it for your house move, you may find yourself rolling it out across other areas of your life.

EXERCISE: CREATE YOUR ACTION STATIONS CHECKLIST

- Write a list of each space and room in the property. Include the garden, under the stairs, loft/attic space, garage.
- Break down each space and room further. For example:

- Repeat this for every space and room in the house so that you have an itemised list of every area in your home that needs attention.
- Allocate a day or time period for each specific area. Don't try and tackle too much in one go. Make it bite-sized and manageable.

- Now, split by person. Who in your household, family circle or wider selling team can sort out these areas? There are more people in this sale than you alone, so use their support.
- For a free, editable list that you can download, head to the online *Happy Home Sale* resource library at natalieevansuk.com

---

Preparing to move: Practical factors

The key to making this checklist work is to take *action*. A list isn't productive if you don't do what you planned to do. Review your checklist. Is it realistic? If so, we can get cracking.

First, there are practical factors that we need to consider to help make everything flow smoothly. Ask yourself the following questions:

- Where are you going to put things once you have sorted them?
- Do you need to book a skip?
- Will you do a trip to a local charity shop or run to the local household waste and recycling centre? Do you know where they are? Are there any restrictions on what items they take?
- What removal support do you need and when? (We will look at removals in more detail later in the chapter.)
- Do you have what you need to begin packing? There is nothing worse than being ready to go and then finding that

you don't have tape or a pen. You will need:

- Various size boxes
- Bubble wrap
- Packing tape
- Marker pens
- Post-it notes
- Fragile tape

You'll find an additional checklist to help you with your planning at the online Happy Home Sale resource library at natalieevansuk.com

Taking time now to identify exactly what you need to do ahead of your move will simplify the final stages of your sale. Fixing times, days and people to tackle each of the areas will minimise the effort, which will make it far more manageable.

Preparing to move: Emotional factors

How are you feeling seeing the list? If you are looking at the number of points and already feeling daunted by the bullet points, then take a moment to pause. Take a deep breath and remember, tackle everything in small steps. Getting fully prepared for your move may take you weeks, even months, so start now and take on each section a small chunk at a time.

Packing your home is not an easy challenge, even for smaller properties. As humans, we are natural hoarders – some may be more extreme than others. Inside every home there are things that we no longer need, things we don't use and things that we can't even remember buying. We get so emotionally connected to these items that we end up with a collection of 'things' that don't have a space or place in our day-to-day lives, but we feel a subconscious duty to keep them.

Emotions may feel more at the forefront when sorting or packing the home of a loved one, especially if they are no longer with us. The fear that their memory will be lost with the items we pass on brings raw pain and emotion. In these cases, take additional time to prepare. Acknowledge and release your emotions. Only once you have dealt with your feelings will you be ready to make the right practical decisions. Be kind to yourself and give yourself time.

The twelve-month rule

Choosing which items to keep, rehome and discard can be tough, but my twelve-month rule is about to change that for you: if you have not used the item for twelve months, then it is unlikely that you will use it again in the twelve months to come. Rehome or discard it.

I recently got chatting to a lady in a co-working space outside of London. She was talking about her struggles with her appearance. While she was happy with how she looked, she felt constantly disappointed that she hadn't got back to her pre-pregnancy clothes size. She explained that she had had a baby boy eighteen months ago and had just moved home, but the constant reminders in her wardrobe of the size she used to be pulled her down every day.

I asked her, 'Why didn't you just throw them away when you moved?', to which she replied, 'Just in case I got back into them.'

I flat-out ban the phrase 'just in case' when working with clients in their preparation to move. I've heard things like:

- 'Just in case the kids want toasties.'
- 'Just in case I get back to a size 12.'
- 'Just in case I start playing golf.'

The 'just in case' mentality will not only see you filling your new home with unnecessary things, but may also prevent you from starting anew. Be firm with yourself. The last thing you want to do is fill your new home with old things. You are about to begin your next chapter, one filled with new light, new space and new opportunity. By discarding or rehoming anything that hasn't served you for the past twelve months, you are giving yourself the clarity and freedom to start a fresh new chapter of your life.

CASE STUDY: GETTING THE RIGHT PERSON TO PACK THE RIGHT ROOM

When I am focused, I can be pretty brutal with clearing out things. There is nothing I love more than spending a Sunday afternoon pulling everything out of the children's wardrobes and getting rid of the pieces that no longer fit. The same applied when we moved home. I made sure that I had a plan to tackle each area, one at a time, until I had rehomed or discarded everything that no longer served a purpose in our life.

My downfall was the garage. The garage has never been an area of the house that I have paid any attention to. Old paint tins, kids' paddling pool, bikes, tools – it was full of things that I have little interest in. But I decided that I would take time to sort through the items to keep, rehome or discard.

I started well. I knew that there was no need for the paint tins, so put them to one side to discard. But the job became more and more taxing.

I was definitely the wrong person for this task. I ended up losing my patience and packing pretty much everything to move, purely because I had no idea.

Most of the items turned out not to be needed and a year after moving, we discovered that one of my garage packing boxes had never been opened. Needless to say, it went straight to the waste centre without even being undone.

The moral of the above story is to make sure that the right people are taking ownership of the right spaces. This ensures that the correct decisions are made. In my case, my overly generous packing meant we ended up moving too much stuff, but on the flip side, getting rid of something you later need may lead to some rather uncomfortable conversations when it is discovered to be missing and is long gone.

Make packing a team sport

No matter what your situation is – a family, a couple or a group of friends – getting everyone involved in sorting, packing and preparing for completion will not only reduce time and pressure, but will bring fun and closure to your selling journey.

While for some, a move is fuelled with excitement, others are pained by loss, separation, unwanted change and grief. The support of a friendly face brings valuable support while working through rooms and boxes full of triggering emotion.

In all moves, the packing process will reveal stories, memories and tales of good and bad times. Times you'll laugh at and times you would rather forget. Having others there to talk through and share these stories will bring reflection and even acceptance.

Creating the space to open up is beneficial to everyone. While this idea may sound like a therapy session, you can inject fun into this and face your memories in a playful manner.

How about holding a packing party? Like a painting party, where friends come to help someone paint a new home, why not host one for packing? This works well for a friend group or a family with older children. You'll get the work done, enjoy the company and stories and celebrate in the process.

You could even play a game or make a competition out of it. Set challenges for people to find things like the most random item, the oldest item, the funniest memory – this can be great fun for all the family. You'll get individuals to take responsibility for their own space and enjoy it along the way.

CASE STUDY: REMEMBERING THE GOOD TIMES

Mr Peters' elderly mother sadly passed away in 2021, leaving behind a wonderfully close family. Her home had always been the hub of their activity. The whole family would be there on a Sunday morning in time for pastries that she had collected from the bakery the day before. Her children, grandchildren and even great-grandchildren would congregate in her tiny front room on the same chairs that had been there for decades, using the same china from her days as a young bride.

The day she passed away, everything in the house looked as it had for decades. The only thing missing was her, but the family still returned. It felt special.

The idea of taking her home apart felt too painful for anyone to consider, but they knew that they needed to part with the house and place it on the market. While there was nothing in the home that the family members wanted to keep, they wanted to remember everything just as it was, the rooms and the atmosphere.

Mr Peters had an idea. He made a plan for the whole family to pack the home together one weekend, but while they did, he recorded it. They laughed, cried, shared memories, played games and remembered stories that they had forgotten about. All the while, everything was captured on video. The family were able to create something that stored their memories but allowed them to release the furniture, items and eventually the house to go on the market.

Mr Peters' solution to help his family navigate this devastating situation was truly beautiful, and is a great suggestion for any family who need to rehome or discard items but are not quite ready to cut the emotional ties with them. It's a simple idea, but one that works so effectively to keep the precious memories safe, when the physical items move on.

Arranging the move

We have focused a lot on identifying pieces that may not serve you moving forward, but what about the things that you want to come with you?

It is important that everything is packed safely, ready to transport to your new home, and knowing your options for this will bring you some ease. Whether opting for a removals service, van hire or self-transport, it is important to figure out exactly what you need early on and get the wheels in motion.

To help you identify what service may best suit your needs, ask the following:

1. Do you want help packing your possessions, or would you prefer to do the packing?
2. Would you feel safer having fragile items packed on your behalf?
3. Do you live close enough to the property to prepare and pack it, or would you benefit from someone else managing it for you?
4. How many items are you moving?
5. Are you able to transport any items yourself?
6. Do you need help taking items downstairs or out of the property?

7. Do you want your possessions to be unpacked and set up, ready for you to move straight in?
8. What is your budget?

If you have few items and are happy to move them yourself, self-packing and van hire may be a good option for you. Hiring a self-drive van can be up to three times cheaper than booking a full removals or 'man and van' service. But doing it yourself is a completely hands-on, physical option.

In many cases, and for larger home moves, a 'man and van' or removals company will be hired to support the workload. Too often, sourcing the right removals team is left right until the last minute, which leaves sellers with limited options on suppliers and availability. Your removals team is a key player in your dream team, so spending time finding the right one to work with you is essential. With thousands of removals suppliers in the UK offering differing levels of service, it can feel daunting to find the team who you can trust to provide the service that you require, to look after you and your treasured belongings.

How to choose your removals supplier

The key to making sure that you get the perfect service is to be open and clear about what you want and need from your removal service from your first enquiry. The prospective supplier should arrange to come out and fully survey the house and your possessions before issuing a quote. Make sure you get a few quotes, giving them all the same information.

It is essential to work with a removals team who not only have a clean van and tidy workforce, but who are capable of responding to change. Change can occur anywhere in a property move, and being aware and prepared for it makes it easier to manage both emotionally and physically. Get clear information from the removals service about how they respond to change, and ask for examples of situations where they have dealt with changes in moving plans, unexpected delays or cancellations. Make sure that you check that they are flexible on date shifts. Knowing that your removals team is on hand to support you whatever happens will bring great relief to you if you do have any adjustments closer to moving day.

Your chosen removal supplier will likely request a deposit to hold a date. While it may not be set in stone for your move, you'll be in a stronger position to avoid completion delays by reserving a potential date ahead of time than doing so at the last minute.

Ahead of putting down a deposit, check their credentials. Your removals team will be handling your most important possessions, so you want to be confident that they are able to do everything they have promised. Just because Auntie Sue knows the removal manager's mother, that doesn't guarantee that their son's company will be the best choice for you. Check their reviews on platforms like Google, Facebook and Check a Trade to be confident that you are in the right hands.

When it comes to speaking with them, here are the key things that you need to ask, discuss and confirm to be sure that your removal supplier is going to look after you:

- Ask for information on insurance
- Ask for confirmation on deposit requirements
- Discuss availability

- Discuss changes to dates and flexibility
- Confirm payment terms and fees

Always follow your intuition. If you feel as though the supplier is avoiding answering or being unclear about any of these details, do not go through with the booking. To make sure that you have the best moving day, you need the best team by your side.

Home-selling Myth 6: Any van will do

Moving home can be an expensive affair and of course, we all strive to find the most cost-effective solutions to bring the numbers down on completion day. But never scrimp on your removal service.

Being the final piece of the puzzle, it is common to see the removals stage as a great opportunity to cut costs at the last hurdle. But this is one area where cutting costs can be risky. Remember, this will be the service moving everything that you have selected as essential to your life. You should never risk the safety of these items for the sake of £50, £100 or even £1,000.

Summary

In this chapter, we have looked at how to tackle your preparation to move. You've created your action stations checklist and know how to plan the tasks and share them with others around you. We have looked at ways to add fun, share memories and even gain self-acceptance during this process as you transition from your past life to your next chapter.

And that's that – you've done it! You have kept focused and worked hard throughout the book and now you are here, ready to go. Your new life is right before you and you are ready to grab hold of it with both hands. You are prepared, you are organised, you are happy and you are here. Today is the day that you have been waiting for. It's the day you move.

Conclusion

Starting a new chapter can feel daunting, exciting and surreal. It's a feeling I am all too familiar with.

In 2019, I was invited to my first Home Staging Association Founding Members meeting. When I arrived at the venue in London, I stood outside to pause and reflect before entering through the large doors. It was worlds away from the small business startup journey that I was just embarking on, and it stirred up a real mixture of excitement, uncertainty and self-doubt.

I made my way up to the office space, which was bustling with an eclectic mix of London professionals going about their day. This was 2019 after all, and there was no sign of the impending pandemic. There I was in my new pair of jeans, crisp white shirt and crimped hair hoping to look the part as I walked into a room full of the home-staging industry's leading professionals.

Being new to the industry, I doubted whether I had anything worthy to contribute to the meeting as discussions centred on the million-pound London apartments that had been staged that month and how the businesses were handling the hundreds of installations per year, all of which was so alien to me. I was an outsider to the hustle and riches of city life.

The conversation turned to working harder and getting the deals. While bigger developers, buy-to-let investors and luxury agents in the city were keeping the established central London staging firms busy, this wasn't translating across the country. The discussion turned to how the smaller staging businesses could sell their services and convert clients by taking a more confident and masculine approach to their sales technique, delivering powerful statistics in a more direct manner. Visions came flashing back of the powerhouse estate agent that I had met back when I was selling our home. I remembered how his technique had made me feel and knew this just wasn't me.

That's when I felt myself begin to talk, not knowing what I was about to say. In a room of established leaders, what did I seriously have to bring to the table?

'Um, I agree in part,' I said. 'But most of the time, I come to client consultations with a packet of tissues and a supportive smile. I find that this approach is most effective for me.'

The table looked at me. It was clear from an immediate glance that 99% of the table thought that I was crazy. The idea of me coming into a sales meeting with a prospective client in a soft and loving manner, armed with tissues rather than swanky digital brochures and powerful statistics, was evidently ludicrous. I immediately felt myself become a little flushed, thinking, *Oh bloody hell, Natalie, what did you say that for?*

From across the table, one kind-eyed member smiled and gave me a nod of support. I later learnt that this was Annie Doherty, international award-winning property expert, industry trainer, author and public speaker. If there was anyone to get a supportive nod from, it was Annie.

I don't know if Annie knew how important that was to me and how it would shape my work within the property industry. Her nod of reassurance has been with me over the past three years, in creating authentic and heartfelt services for my client, in keeping me true to my unconventional yet core values, and in writing this book for you.

Needless to say, I still take tissues and a supportive smile to every home-staging client meeting. There is such power in being kind and supportive to others and to oneself, and through each chapter of this book, I have brought this supportive presence to you, so you can achieve the happiest home sale and onward journey.

I'm sad that we are ending this journey together, but I am so proud of how far you have come. Think back to the negative thoughts and stories that suffocated your understanding of the home-selling journey and compare it to the way you feel today. You are supported, you are worthy and you will achieve everything you desire. You have learnt that selling your home does not have to be the most stressful time of your life – not when you know how to create a happy home sale.

EXERCISE: ONE FINAL ACTIVITY

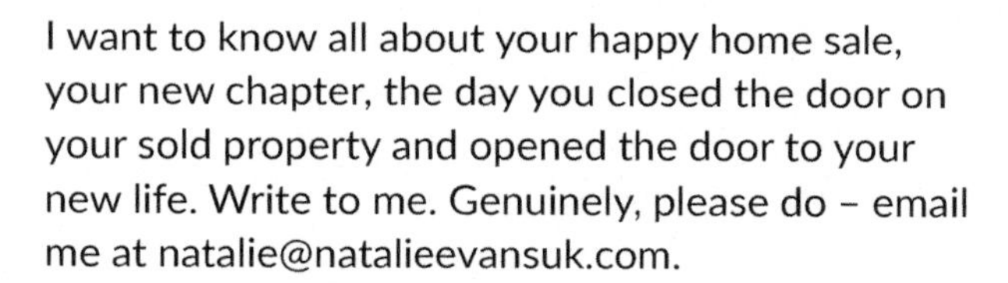

I want to know all about your happy home sale, your new chapter, the day you closed the door on your sold property and opened the door to your new life. Write to me. Genuinely, please do - email me at natalie@natalieevansuk.com.

Thank you for allowing me to be part of your journey and letting me share my lessons, love and support as you have navigated your way to your next chapter.

Kindest wishes,
Natalie

Jargon Buster

Broker (also known as mortgage broker): A broker reviews a client's current financial situation and confirms the amount a mortgage provider will lend them based on their income and outgoings. While a broker may not advise you on your personal finances, they will be able to find a selection of mortgage products from their panel of lenders, and compare the available rates, which are often exclusive to them.

Buyer's market: When there are more homes on offer than there are buyers to buy them, so buyers are at an advantage.

Chain: The number of people/properties dependent on the sale of a home.

Completion: When funds are received by all the correct parties and ownership of a home passes from the seller to the buyer.

Conveyancer (also known as a property solicitor): The solicitor or conveyancer is responsible for managing the process of transferring property from one owner to another. They validate funds, check property details by raising searches and draw up legal contracts for the sale.

Covenant: A specific clause written into the deed or other agreements such as leases, which can impact the direction of a sale.

Deed: The legal document that shows the owner of a property, along with any specific responsibilities or covenants.

Deposit: A monetary commitment to purchase made by a buyer at the point of exchanging contracts.

Energy Performance Certificate (EPC): This is an assessment completed by a professional assessor concerning the energy efficiency and environmental impact of the property. The certificate grades the property from A (best) to G (worst), and suggests follow-up actions to save energy and decrease environmental damage.

Equity: The amount of value that a homeowner holds in a property.

Exchange of contracts: The moment that a buyer and seller formally sign the contracts to buy and sell a property. This is the point that deposits are paid, usually via the solicitor.

Financial advisor: A financial advisor reviews your personal finances and advises on your situation and options. (See also 'Independent financial advisor' below.)

First-time buyer: Someone who is purchasing a property for the first time.

Freehold: The owner of a freehold property owns the building and land that it is built on.

Gazumping: When a higher offer from another buyer is accepted by a seller after they accepted a previous offer.

Gazundering: When a buyer lowers their offer at the end of the selling journey, forcing the seller to accept a lower price.

Home stager: A home stager is an expert in making sure that a property is presented in the best way for going on the market.

Home staging: The act of preparing your property to go on the market for sale or rent.

Independent financial advisor (IFA): An independent financial advisor reviews your personal finances and advises on your situation and options. They provide independent advice which isn't restricted to a set panel of financial suppliers.

Interest rate: The amount you are charged to take out a loan. Usually it is expressed as a percentage of the total amount. A 1% interest rate means that for every pound you borrow, a penny is charged on top.

Land and Buildings Transaction Tax: A cost applied to the purchase of a property in Scotland, based on its value. This replaced Stamp Duty in Scotland in 2015.

Land registry: A database showing all property and land in England and Wales with their registered owners.

Land Transaction Tax: A cost applied to the purchase of property in Wales, based on its value. This replaced Stamp Duty in Wales in 2018.

Leasehold: The owner of a leasehold property owns the building but not the land that it is built on or building that it is situated in. This is common for apartments and flats within blocks. Leasehold properties are often subject to additional leasehold agreements and service charges.

Mortgage: The borrowing of funds from a mortgage lender or bank to make a property purchase.

Mortgage in principle (also known as an agreement in principle, decision in principle or mortgage promise): Confirmation from your mortgage lender on how much they estimate that you can borrow. Your mortgage lender can provide this as written confirmation to prove that you have funds in place to purchase a property.

New build: A property that has recently been built and is yet to be lived in.

Seller's market: When there are more buyers looking for properties than properties available on the market, so sellers are at an advantage.

Sold Subject to Contract (SSTC): This term is often used on online property platforms to show that an offer has been accepted, but no formal contracts have yet been exchanged.

Stamp Duty Land Tax: A cost applied to the purchase of a property in England and Northern Ireland, based on its value.

Surveyor: A surveyor carries out a detailed inspection of a property's condition.

Target buyer: The anticipated buyer type or profile to whom you are marketing your property.

Under offer: This term is often used on online property platforms to show that an offer has been made, but not formally accepted and no contracts exchanged.

Valuation: The estimated value of a property based on its specification, location and neighbourhood sales statistics.

Vendor: Seller.

Acknowledgements

There is always more than one person behind a book, and I couldn't finish mine without a few messages of thanks.

First, to my three children, Olive, Edie and Rory, thank you for understanding the times that I have needed a little extra quiet and for listening to me read paragraphs back to you time and time again.

To my book coach, Monique, who listened to my thoughts and stories and helped me create a coherent book structure.

To the team at Caffè Nero in Whiteley, Hampshire, whose corner hideaway seat and perfectly made flat white has fuelled every chapter in this book.

To my team at Little Barn Door, who have been there from the start through to making this book a reality.

Finally, to my husband, Gareth, who encouraged me from the moment I told him that I wanted to write this book. Thank you for taking over the morning school runs so that I could write, and for staying up after dark to read and edit night after night.

Thank you.

The Author

Natalie Evans is the founding director of the award-winning home-staging specialist Little Barn Door. Since establishing her business in late 2018, Natalie has touched the lives of homeowners across the UK with her unique and inspiring approach to home staging and property sales.

The Little Barn Door brand has quickly grown as news of their clients' successes spread. To date, 80% of the properties worked on by

Natalie and her team have achieved an offer in less than four weeks.

Natalie has been featured in several publications, including *Beautiful South* and *Homes North Magazines,* as well as guest appearances on industry podcasts and BBC Radio. As a founding member of the Home Staging Association UK & Ireland, Natalie is shaping the UK property industry and is determined to introduce the power of mindful preparation and home staging across the UK.

Natalie enjoys walks on the beach or stomping through woodlands with her husband and three children. Away from her home on the south coast of England, Natalie's heart lies in Aberporth on the west coast of Wales, where the air feels fresher and the sun sets later.

Keep in touch.

natalieevansuk.com

@iamnatalieevansuk

@natalieevansuk

@natalieevansuk

Printed in Great Britain
by Amazon